T0360981

UNDERSTANDING RESIDENTIAL CHILD CARE

Understanding Residential Child Care

Nick Frost, Sue Mills and Mike Stein

Routledge
Taylor & Francis Group

LONDON AND NEW YORK

First published 1999 by Ashgate Publishing

Reissued 2018 by Routledge
2 Park Square, Milton Park, Abingdon, Oxon, OX14 4RN
52 Vanderbilt Avenue, New York, NY 10017

Routledge is an imprint of the Taylor & Francis Group, an informa business

Notice:
Product or corporate names may be trademarks or registered trademarks, and are used only for identification and explanation without intent to infringe.

Publisher's Note
The publisher has gone to great lengths to ensure the quality of this reprint but points out that some imperfections in the original copies may be apparent.

Disclaimer
The publisher has made every effort to trace copyright holders and welcomes correspondence from those they have been unable to contact.

A Library of Congress record exists under LC control number: 98035472

ISBN 13: 978-1-138-37024-1 (hbk)
ISBN 13: 978-0-429-42810-4 (ebk)

Contents

Introduction

This book has been written against a background of a crisis of confidence in residential child care. To the public, fed on a diet of scandal, children's homes are places where children are either victims, being physically or sexually abused, or villains, who are beyond control, involved in prostitution, crime or going missing.

To many of those working in the system – residential carers, field social workers and managers – homes can be perceived variously as ineffective, lacking purpose and, compared to foster care and other services, very expensive to run. The rationale for residential child care is perceived to be at best pragmatic and negative ('there is no alternative'), or a place of last resort.

To those resident in children's homes, recent research (Sinclair and Gibbs 1998) suggests that a majority of young people would prefer to have remained at home or to have been looked after somewhere other than their current children's home. This view is often supported by their parents.

Against this negative background it is perhaps not surprising that the numbers in residential child care have decreased dramatically since the late 1970s – from about 29,000 young people in 1979 to around 5,500 in 1996 – and fundamental questions are being raised about the future of residential child care:

- Do we need children's homes at all?
- How did their history contribute to their current form?
- Can they become a positive choice?
- How should they be organised and managed?
- What should residential staff actually do?

1

This book attempts to explore these questions by providing an overview of residential child care linking historical, theoretical, policy, managerial and practice perspectives. Our motivation in writing this book is threefold.

First, our experience in talking to young people, working in and managing residential units, and in research and training, has left us with a commitment to residential child care. It potentially has a positive role to play in our services for looked-after children, but may require radical change to reach this position.

Second, we believe that residential care needs to be understood holistically. By this we mean that history, social theory, politics and theories of collective and individual change all have something to contribute to our understanding of and practice in residential child care.

Third, we are committed to the concept of empowerment as a model for child welfare practice. In this book we intend to explore and develop this concept as a managerial and practice tool for all those engaged in residential child care. Whether these ambitious goals are achieved is for the reader to judge.

Practitioners in residential child care settings may wish to use the book in two ways. First, it provides a context for their practice. Some of the chapters, particularly the historical and theoretical ones, may initially seem to be a long way from day-to-day practice in a children's home. However, these chapters play the role of providing a context for practice by helping to explain where the current practices and ideas have come from and attempt to provide wider explanations for the development of caring institutions. These chapters also attempt to provide connections with everyday practice – connections which attempt to explain some of the current issues and dilemmas facing residential child care. Second, the book also provides a framework for direct practice, both in relation to the management of units and work with children and young people.

Managers of residential child care services should also find the book of use. We attempt to make links between our historical and theoretical context and the more direct application of ideas and concepts to the management of units. We pay particular attention to managerial skills in the residential child care context as we believe that these are fundamental to laying the basis for successful child care practice.

Academics, students and trainers may also find the book helpful in a variety of ways. We do not set out to provide a training pack (see Frost and Harris 1996) as such but the ideas will again provide the historical and theoretical context for the development of input to residential child care practitioners and managers.

Empowering practice – the key concept

There are a number of reasons why we have chosen in this book to make *empowerment* a key connecting idea.

First, we see empowerment as immediately raising political questions about the distribution of power. This provides some distance between our approach, which we hope is informed by political discourse, and what we might identify as 'technicist' or 'professional' discourses which tend to assume that the residential task is simply about 'caring' or improving the quality of the service. Such approaches, we argue, fail to make the necessary connections with the historical and theoretical issues we have raised. For example, it would be easy to dismiss our historical chapter as only of the most obscure academic interest. To take this position, we would argue, is to underestimate the impact of the past on the present. In his studies of many of our major institutions (the prison and the mental hospital, for example) the late French theorist, Michel Foucault, argued for what he called a history of the present. By this we interpret Foucault as meaning that we need to understand the way that the present has been constructed by our historical past. For example, Chapter 1 outlines the crucial role of the 'less eligibility' principle of the Poor Law on residential care. We would argue that 'the long shadow' of 'less eligibility' is still cast over residential child care and that this helps to explain some of the tensions between 'care' and 'control' which residential practitioners face in their everyday practice, as well as a context for understanding contemporary forms of abuse.

Second, empowerment provides for us what we might call a 'practice template', or a method of assessing the impact and consistency of our practice. This idea is quite easy to apply: for instance, we can ask whether a given practice or policy is empowering to children and young people or not? As we will see in Chapter 3, on direct work with children and young people, we conceptualise this as a more complex idea than 'promoting the best interests of the child'. It is certainly more subtle than a straightforward emphasis on 'children's rights' as an organising concept, for empowerment has to address the individual disadvantages experienced by many children and young people as a consequence of their damaging and disruptive pre-care experiences. We argue then that empowerment can be used to assess the impact of practice and to provide a clear conceptual framework for both the practice and management of residential child care.

Third, empowerment is also capable of providing a practice basis for management. For children and young people to be empowered it is also important for staff to be empowered. In fact we will argue that this is a prerequisite for children and young people to be empowered. For this reason we place a strong emphasis on the importance of management and management skills in this book.

Fourth, and finally, we argue that empowerment, as a profoundly political concept, is capable of recognising the differential distribution of power according to gender, generation, class, ethnicity, sexuality and disability. A practice model, based on challenging the inequality arising out of these differences, is therefore placed centre stage. To ensure that this happens we would argue that a theoretical and historical perspective is required which can take into account the significance of these social differences in residential child care.

It is for these reasons that we see empowerment as the central organising concept of our book.

The structure of the book

Chapter 1 examines the history of British residential child care, beginning with an examination of the roots of welfare provision for the poor and vagrant and assessing the development of more specialist provision for children and young people. We then move on to examine the impact of the Poor Law which stamped the stigma of the workhouse on much subsequent provision of residential child care. The analysis then looks at the key role played by Victorian philanthropic organisations – analysing the role of religion, the importance of theories of urban degeneration, the practice of child migration. The chapter then goes on to examine the post-war period beginning with the Children Act 1948 and the key landmarks of the Children and Young Persons Act 1969, and then subsequent legislation. It will be argued that during the 1960s a complex interplay of permanence theories, familial ideology and the move towards 'non-institutional' care created the seeds of the crisis in residential care in the 1980s. The analysis will close with the lead up to the Children Act 1989 and the 'Pindown', 'Beck' and other scandals.

Chapter 2 examines some of the key 'macro-theories' which can be applied to residential provision. This discussion provides a context for our later, more practice-based discussion. The chapter begins by analysing in detail some established theoretical frameworks including the work of Erving Goffman, whose important theories of residential settings applied to total institutions such as mental hospitals, and have been influential in the critique of all residential settings. This section will examine the value of Goffman's thinking, and its influence, as well as providing a critique of Goffman's work. We then analyse some of the work of the French theorist Michel Foucault which has been influential in many areas of social analysis. Whilst he did not write specifically about social care settings, his analysis of disciplinary regimes and discourse have a lot to teach us about residential child care. We will then explore analyses of residential child care which have seen it has the extension of the workhouse and have conceptualised residential child care as having a social control role. These theories tend to emphasise class and poverty as the key elements in understanding residential care.

Having provided an overview and critique of various theoretical frameworks we will then go on to develop a framework of our own. This will draw on elements of the theories already mentioned but will have as its central theme an attempt to understand residential child care as a complex interplay of class, gender, generation and ethnic difference. The insights of feminist theory, particularly around theories of state/family relations will also be utilised. Central to our theory, and laying the foundations for the later practice element of the book, will be an exploration of the concept of *power* and how the concept of *empowerment* suggests a coherent framework for a progressive theory and practice.

Chapter 3 will explore how the concept of empowerment can be applied to working with children and young people in residential child care settings. The chapter will examine the concept of children's rights, the applicability of this concept in residential child care and a critical reflection on the theory and practice associated with this concept. This will be followed by an exploration of the concept of empowerment and a discussion of the detailed practical application of the concept, including the involvement of children and young people in all levels of decision making. Particular attention will be paid to issues arising for young people in relation to the diverse backgrounds of accommodated young people: black and white, male and female, the victims of abuse, offenders and those presenting challenging behaviours.

In Chapter 4 we explore the significance of the Children Act 1989, which provides the current legal and regulative framework in which English and Welsh residential child care exists. This chapter will examine the content of, and issues raised by, the Children Act. Part of the new agenda in residential child care is an increased emphasis on 'quality' and the mechanics of inspection and registration. The concept of quality will be explored including an explanation of the role of quality assurance, quality control mechanisms and complaints and representations procedures will be explored. A framework for developing forms which emphasise user participation and empowerment will be proposed.

In Chapter 5 we explore the practice of management in residential child care, drawing on the theoretical, historical and policy base which we have already mentioned. It will be argued that forms of residential child care which empower young people are crucially dependent on management systems which support and develop staff teams and individuals. The next chapter, Chapter 6, will explore systems of staff development and supervision. These specific management functions provide a crucial underpinning in ensuring high quality practice in residential child care.

Chapter 7 centres on the issue of abuse in residential child care, which has been crucial in stimulating the current level of interest in residential child care. How can we prevent children and young people being abused in residential child care settings? In addressing this question this chapter will pursue two main lines of inquiry: first a conceptual exploration of different forms of abuse in residential child care based upon recent scandals, and second a consideration of the context in which this has arisen, including the low and marginal status of residential child care.

Chapter 8 looks at the issue of young people leaving residential care, an issue which has all too often been underplayed by the theory and practice of residential child care. Using recent research the chapter will illustrate how preparation for independence should be an integral part of empowering residential child care practice.

Our final chapter, Chapter 9, will argue that a positive future for residential child care is possible but is dependent on understanding the place of residential provision coherently and providing empowering regimes. Concrete policy and practice proposals for the further development of residential child care will be put forward. This will focus on strategies for addressing residential practice in relation to the diverse range of young people in residential settings.

1   A history of residential child care

Introduction

In this chapter we wish to provide an historical analysis of residential child care in England and Wales. This is important not only to give us a perspective on the contemporary state of residential child care but also because residential child care very much bears the marks of its history – indeed it can be argued that the history of residential child care has been a dialogue with the past and, more specifically, with its Poor Law roots. This history will be analysed in five periods: pre-1597, 1597 until 1834, 1834 until 1908, 1908 until 1939 and post-1939.

For each period key themes will be identified which we argue form the central developments during that period. The issue of power and empowerment is central here. How was power exercised through the formation of the first institutions? What was the impact of this exercise of power on those who were resident? What does this history suggest about shifts in the exercise of power and about contemporary possibilities?

Origins: before 1597

Key themes:
- The development of specialist provision for children developing from undifferentiated reactions to the poor and the vagrant;
- The development of a range of residential provision including hospitals, workhouses and boarding-out provision operated both by the State and private individuals;

- The central place of work training for young people, which was perceived as a solution to pauperism.

We begin with an examination of the place of child welfare in the pre-Reformation period. Jean Heywood has suggested that there existed a network of support for the orphaned and illegitimate child – being cared for within communities or by a network of charitable provision: 'Yet while he was nobody's child, he was also the child of the people, and some community obligation was implied towards him' (Heywood 1978: 1). The child was integrated into the community and the focus of life was around the village and the settlement rather than around the family and household: 'In the fact that life was centred round the community rather than the family there lay the possibility of opportunity and protection for the unwanted child' (Heywood 1978: 8).

As the pace of social change began to quicken and social disruption followed the State began to take a more active role both in relation to attempting to regulate the labour market and to provide for those not in work.

The history of state welfare has long been concerned with regulating the perceived threat posed by the poor and dispossessed. Fear of this group led to the Statute of Labourers 1351, in an attempt to control the wages of labourers (Fraser 1973: 28). This Statute was later strengthened by the Poor Law Act of 1388, which sought to limit labour mobility and the threat of the vagrant. Throughout the fourteenth and fifteenth century children and young people were seen simply as *part of* this general concern with the poor and the threat of disorder. Thus even the Poor Law of 1531 had made no specific mention of children and young people. By 1536, however, we begin to see the emergence of specific provision for children and young people – the authorities were enabled to apprentice vagrant children, aged between 5 and 14, so that they would be able to learn a trade. This was an educative model which was designed to train and crucially *rescue* children from a future of vagrancy. Those aged 12 to 16 who refused such training, or who returned to begging, could be physically punished – thus providing a coercive back-up for the educative ideal. Parish officers who did not implement these provisions could themselves be put in the stocks for two days (Pinchbeck and Hewitt 1969: 95). The Act also introduced the idea of children being put out, or 'boarded out', with wet nurses. Additionally parishes were empowered by the Act to collect money for the relief of paupers – perhaps the first recognition of some state responsibility for the poor.

Meanwhile, as a result of the economic dislocation of the period, social unrest grew and eventually provided the conditions for the passage of the Poor Law Act of 1547. The Act allowed for the children of established vagrants to be taken into the apprenticeship of any citizen who presented before a constable, two neighbours and a Justice; an apprenticeship could last until the age of 20 for a young woman, and 24 for a young man. This again reinforces one of the main aims of sixteenth-century intervention – the emphasis on work and the development of skills to save children and young people from pauperism. If the young person attempted to run away they could be put in chains and used effectively as a slave. The promotion of parish apprenticeship remained a central thread of the legislation of the seventeenth and eighteenth centuries, but the idea was undermined in practice and by the variations which existed in local practice. The Act of 1547 proved to be unworkable and was reformed in 1549 to include the provision that vagrant parents could lose their parental rights – a theme of child welfare which was to survive until the passage of the Children Act 1989. Whilst the apprenticeship provisions continued, the 1549 Act also repealed the provisions which allowed for children to be used as slave labour. Interestingly some concept of the welfare of the child was introduced, so that complaints by two honest neighbours that the treatment of an apprenticed child was 'unreasonable in ordering and bringing up the child' could result in the apprenticeship being discharged and the child being placed with a new master.

During this period we also see the emergence of charitable residential provision aimed specifically at children. The City of London concluded an agreement in 1552 to operate four hospitals to administer to the needs of the destitute poor and beggars. Two hospitals were designed for the aged and sick, Christ's Hospital was for children and the notorious Bridewell for reforming the vagrant and idle.

Here we see the emerging emphasis on child welfare. The key aim of the newly formed institution was to care for and to educate the vagrant child, with the aim of ensuring that they were educated and later able to pursue a trade. During 1552 almost a thousand children were so accommodated and cared for. It is important to note at this stage that the later idea of 'less eligibility' was not in play. The administrators of the new hospitals went to some lengths to ensure that the hospitals were adequately furnished and equipped. However, the Christ's Hospital for children was soon overstretched, although it had been originally designed to cope with all the destitute children of the capital. Pinchbeck and Hewitt (1969) suggest that this pressure may have been the result of a 1557 equivalent of the Child Support Act, enforcing support from putative fathers. They suggest that this led to an increase in children being abandoned, some of whom ended up in Christ's Hospital. Whatever the causes, as a result of the pressure on places the hospital reformed its policy so that only children born within wedlock were admitted, except in the most extreme cases.

Another problem was that given the quality and quantity of provision in London there was a danger that London could act as a magnet for the poor and dispossessed, as little provision existed in the rest of the country.

Partly as a result of state and philanthropic initiatives, the needs of children and young people were increasingly recognised as being specific and specialised. The Poor Law Act of 1572 introduced the first distinction between younger children and youth. Young people over 14 involved in unlicensed begging could be imprisoned until the next session and subjected to the same punishment as adults. The exception to this was if someone could be found to apprentice them. In contrast, children under 14 were to be dealt with, presumably by what was regarded as the more liberal technique, by being whipped or placed in the stocks if found to be involved in unlicensed begging. Thus by the end of the sixteenth century we see the emergence of specialist residential provision for children and young people both in the state and philanthropic sector.

What we have seen is the inherent tension between 'care' and 'control' – an expressed wish to improve the condition of pauperised children and young people, which exists side by side with punishment, control and containment. This tension lies at the heart of residential provision for children and young people.

Consolidation – 1597–1833

Key themes:
- A shift in attitudes towards the poor child which set the scene for 'less eligibility' and the 1834 Poor Law Amendment Act;
- The development of a system of provision for children which varied considerably across the country;
- The development of residentially based workhouse provision operating alongside apprenticeship and boarding out for children and young people.

The landmark which signifies the commencement of our second period is the passage of the Act for the Relief of the Poor in 1597, a piece of legislation which was largely re-enacted in 1601, and became the basis of provision until the passage of the Poor Law Amendment Act of 1834.

Again the primary concern of this legislation was with vagrancy. The preamble to the 1597 Statute puts the point succinctly:

> of late years more than in time past there have been sundry towns, parishes and houses of husbandry destroyed and become desolate, whereof a great number of poor people are become wanderers, idle and loose, which is the cause of infinite inconvenience. [Bruce 1968: 36]

The 1597 Act appointed overseers of the poor, whose role was the 'setting to work of the children of all such whose parents shall not be thought able to keep and maintain their children', to provide materials to 'set the poor to work on', and to provide 'the necessary relief of the lame, impotent, old, blind and such other being poor and not able to work' (Bruce 1968: 32). Additionally the Act provided for the 'putting out of such Children to be Apprentices, to be gathered out of the same Parish, according to the Ability of the same Parish' (quoted in Heywood 1978: 10n). The primary responsibility for children, however, was clearly perceived as remaining with the family: the means test had its roots in these provisions, namely that 'the parents or children of every poor and impotent person, being of sufficient ability, shall at their own charge relieve and maintain every such poor person.'

The 1597 Act made a distinction between three classes of pauper:

- the impotent to be placed in abiding places, later known as poorhouses
- the able-bodied unemployed, later to be placed in workhouses
- and the recalcitrant idle who were to be sent to houses of correction.

In theory this classification was crucial to the Poor Law, but in practice it was more practical for the Poor Law authorities locally to place all three groups together in the unified workhouse. The workhouse established by this Act can be seen as the first attempt by the state to provide residential accommodation for children and young people. As we have seen this initiative is closely linked with some dominant ideas and ideologies: the fear and the threat of the dispossessed poor; a particular attempt to regulate the mobility of these groups; the close association between economic status and the loss of what we would now call civil rights, including 'parental rights', and the attempt of the state to intervene to resolve the social problems which were presented. The fact that the expenses of operating the 1601 Act came from the rates meant that, at least to some extent 'in principle the State accepted the responsibility for securing the proper treatment and training of children by those into whose care the law had entrusted them' (Pinchbeck and Hewitt 1969: 98).

The 1601 Act was unable however to provide a comprehensive solution to the scale of social disruption of the period. As Clegg states, 'flight out of feudal relations could only be flight into urban centres or into vagrancy. There was nowhere else to go' (1989: 244). Thus in 1609 another major theme of child welfare emerges – the idea of migration to the colonies. Pinchbeck and Hewitt report that the Privy Council suggested that the Corporation of London should raise money to send the poor to Virginia. Whilst nothing seems to have happened immediately, the idea re-emerged in 1617, and in 1619 one hundred children were sent to Virginia. The children were to be set to work as apprentices until the age of 21, after which they would be rented some land on which to work. The exercise was repeated, on slightly reformed conditions, in 1620 and on many occasions subsequently. A further solution was enacted in the Act of 1703 – an Act which allowed for boys aged 10 or more who were beggars or whose parents were a charge on the parish to be apprenticed into the navy. This practice seems to have continued throughout much of the eighteenth century. A further Act of 1717 allowed for young people aged 15–18 to be transported to North America for up to eight years. As we shall see later such practices relating to migration existed until the 1960s. In attempting to understand the appeal of the migration policy we must try to understand the ideas which influenced the policy. Primary amongst these was that children can be reformed by the countryside and fresh air, that indigenous poverty can be 'solved' by such solutions, and that children had a better chance of success if separated from the environment, and the people, including their parents, who had contributed to their 'downfall'. Further, the children and young people were seen as a supply of labour, thus serving the needs of the 'mother' country.

Meanwhile during this period we also saw the growth and the consolidation of the movement to provide specific targeted workhouse provision for children and young people. The period leading up to the passage of the infamous Poor Law Amendment Act of 1834 witnessed the widespread development of work-houses, outdoor relief schemes and the boarding out of children. This was a complex system which was largely dependent on the initiatives and whims of local officers and activists and, therefore, defies straightforward analysis. Fraser has argued that, at the end of the eighteenth century, 'No contemporary then (and no historian since) was conversant with the whole nationally varying system' (1973: 32).

The later half of the seventeenth century saw the growth of a number of workhouse systems, some of a generic nature and others designed specifically for children. Cities such as London and Bristol developed workhouse systems designed for children, sometimes based on a partnership between the parish and local philanthropists. These patchy and sporadic developments were encouraged by the Poor Law Relief Act of 1722 which gave parishes permissive powers to provide workhouses and to apply the workhouse test – that is, those who refused to stay in the workhouse would not be entitled to outdoor relief.

This State provision went hand-in-hand with private provision. Neither the State sector nor what we would now call the voluntary sector had a monopoly of provision. In 1741 Thomas Coram established his Foundling Hospital, in London's Conduit Fields, often identified as the first residential children's establishment. Coram was determined to eradicate the problem of abandoned babies in the streets of London, a result of the deprivation of the period and of punitive attitudes toward children born out of wedlock. The hospital itself seems to have been humanely run and many children were fostered out to the countryside. As Fildes has established:

> At first, the hospital employed only two wet nurses, and in the first three months 90 foundlings were taken in at a rate of 30 a month. These were assigned to dry or wet nurses, with over two-thirds being fed by hand. The relative mortality was 19% in the case of the wet nursed, and 53% of those dry nursed. (1988: 160)

This led to the development of approved, supervised and country-based wet nurses.

Meanwhile in the crowded workhouses there was also a high death rate. In 1757 Hanway began to visit all the London workhouses to record the death rates in each establishment (apparently hoping to encourage competition to improve these figures – a modern idea indeed). Hanway's work helped to contribute to the passage of the 1767 Act which required workhouses to record all relevant information as part of the attempt to improve standards. In particular, Hanway was keen to stimulate boarding out – thus introducing the now familiar rivalry between foster and residential care. Parishes were obliged to send all children under 6 to be fostered in the countryside, within two weeks after being born or entering the workhouse. This included a payment system to foster mothers, which encouraged them to keep the child well and healthy, and a system of visiting which foreshadowed the role of the contemporary social worker.

Similar developments were happening in the state sector again reflecting the interplay between the two sectors. In 1774 in Sheffield the Guardians began to develop cottage homes for children – smaller units which attempted to reduce the impact of large institutions on children. However, it remained the case that most children were housed in the general workhouses, where they faced the problems of institutionalisation and mixing with a wide range of the destitute and dispossessed.

Those children who were apprenticed also faced many difficulties during the late seventeenth and early eighteenth century. They were often forced to endure the degradation and exploitation of industrial labour. The 1802 Preservation of the Health and Morals of Apprentices and others Employed in Cotton and other Mills contained provision to protect parish apprentices from these excesses. The Act separated accommodation for boys and girls, limited the number to sleep in one bed and attempted to improve working conditions (see Heywood 1978).

While provision varied across the country, there was undoubtedly a shift to more punitive attitudes towards such children and young people between the sixteenth and eighteenth centuries. As Pinchbeck and Hewitt point out:

18th century accounts of the children's workhouse movement bear eloquent testimony of the deterioration in social attitudes towards the children of the poor since the sixteenth century...economy in relation to the children of the poor became the dominant idea in the minds of most administrators, and persisted until the early nineteenth century, when it was seen at its worst in connection with the principle of 'less eligibility'. (1969: 175)

If this analysis is correct what we witnessed during this period was a shift in the 'care' and 'control' couplet towards the control side. Far from being empowered and enabled to take more control over their lives, children and young people were more controlled, more and more the subjects of harsh judgmental regimes.

The dominance of 'less eligibility': 1834–1908

Key themes :
* The parallel development of the state and philanthropic sectors;
* The emergence of the domestic ideal as a model for child welfare;
* The dominance of child rescue and the separation of children from their parents.

The state sector

The Poor Law Amendment Act of 1834 marks a significant point in the development of residential provision for children. In this section we will examine developments in the state sector under the Act and the parallel developments in the philanthropic sector.

The Industrial Revolution brought with it social and economic upheaval, which had an impact on the way children were perceived and responded to. In 1834 Poor Law Amendment Act led to the formation of parish unions and a growth in the number of residential establishments – most of these were 'multi-purpose' workhouses where all paupers were housed together, including children and young people. These establishments were firmly based on the principle of 'less eligibility', where efficiency and economy were the watchwords. The Act also stimulated the growth of philanthropic schools for poor, handicapped children, by enabling Guardians to pay fees to accommodate and school these children and young people.

The harsh conditions and mixing of inmates in the workhouses led one group of observers to comment in 1852 that they 'had seen nothing in the prisons and lunatic asylums of Europe to equal conditions in the English workhouse, where children, lunatics, incorrigible, innocent, old, disabled were all mixed together' (Webb 1910: 88).

How did these developments impact on the care of children and young people? One policy pursued by the Poor Law Commissioners was to work towards the separation of children from adults in workhouses and the provision of specific services for children. In 1835 the Commissioners established regulations to ensure that all workhouse children received three hours of education per day, and that schoolmasters and schoolmistresses were appointed to this end. The initiative again raised the recurrent theme of provision for pauper children – the emphasis was on education in the hope that this would lead children out of pauperism and into employment. This educational initiative faced some problems: the ghettoisation of children in workhouse settings was not a sound basis for educational development. Partially in response to this in 1846 the Commissioners appointed Inspectors to try to ensure the development of national standards and to tackle the problem of local variability.

Alongside these educational developments there was increasing concern about the treatment of apprentices, who were in danger of being abused or exploited in their apprenticeship settings. These concerns led to the development of stronger educational policies by the Commissioners.

From 1849 on there was an emphasis on the development of separate residential schools for children. These were usually the product of unions of Poor Law Boards, and situated in the country. The idea was to promote the education of children and to gain the benefits of country environments, particularly away from the influence of 'demoralised' adult paupers. However, these schools, whilst favoured during the 1850s and 1860s were always struggling against the odds, and were soon to be discredited by the lack of achievement and outbreaks of opthalmia in the schools. In 1873 Mrs Nassau Senior was asked by the Commissioners to inquire into the education of pauper girls. She too was critical of the system:

> The massing of the girls together in large numbers was bad and must issue in failure; that their physical condition when in the schools and their moral condition on leaving them was disappointing and unsatisfactory; and that, while the scholastic training of both boys and girls in the Metropolitan pauper schools was first rate, on all other points the system of education did not answer in the case of girls, even at the very best separate and district schools, and that many of them were, in general intelligence, below children of the same class educated at home. (quoted by Heywood 1978: 72)

The 1870 Education Act allowed for compulsory education for all children, so that workhouse children could attend mainstream local schools. The impact of the Act and Mrs Senior's report led to the decline of the district schools and an increased emphasis on boarding out and the renewed development of cottage homes.

The Poor Law authorities were determined to separate children from the demoralising influences of the older paupers in order to give them a chance of escaping from pauperism. The newly emerging strategy was based on the principle of attempting to reduce the impact of institutionalisation on children and young people. Boarding out was seen to be particularly appropriate for orphans and those separated from their parents. However, there were limitations to this policy: there had been examples of abuse by foster parents and there was a limit to the number of suitable foster parents, especially during times of economic distress. Fostering was also not considered suitable for those with contact with their parents or for children who spent short periods in and out of the workhouse. Most unions therefore worked on a dual-track policy of developing boarding out alongside residential provision. Again we shall see later that some of these issues remain with us today.

Cottage homes, which had been favoured earlier in the century, were challenged along some of the same lines that the district schools had been: they were too large, encouraged institutionalisation and gathered large numbers of pauper children together. Many unions therefore shifted towards smaller, scattered, homes, which attempted to be as close as possible to an idealised model of family life. The Local Government Board, which had taken over from the Poor Law Commissioners, examined the developments of the cottage homes in the voluntary sector. They reported on Princess Mary's Village home, for example, 'the unit is adopted for the family is ten…the whole system being based on the family group, the housemothers are the pivot on which it turns' (Heywood 1978: 74). This admiration of the family group system was to be contrasted with the workhouse system where the children's' minds 'are contracted and their affections stifled', as a report of 1861 stated. The momentum was therefore behind the scattered home, which was later to provide the model for the Family Group Home of the twentieth century. Here we have a major theme of the development of residential care: to what degree could residential child care re-create the positive aspects of family life? This will form a major theme of our study.

The philanthropic sector

There developed in the second half of the nineteenth century the basis of the major philanthropic child welfare organisations which still dominate the sector today: Dr Barnardo's (now Barnardo's), National Children's Homes (now NCH – Action for Children), the Waifs and Strays Society (now the Children's Society) and the National Society for the Prevention of Cruelty to Children (NSPCC). This sector grew independently, but in close relation to the state sector. The organisations which mainly concern us in the context of this study of residential child care are Barnardo's, National Children's Homes and the

Waif and Strays Society, all of which developed extensive residential provision. We shall examine the main features of these organisations, and, for illustrative purposes, will draw on the example of Barnardo's.

We can identify two main factors which these organisations shared. First, they were largely based in religious motivation – indeed the Waif and Strays were attached closely to the Church of England and the National Children's Homes to the Methodists. Though Barnardo's was largely the inspiration of one man, he too was motivated by religious, not to say, evangelical motivations. As Parker points out: 'The impact of religious beliefs upon Victorian child care can hardly be over-estimated' (1990: 12).

Second, these were rescue organisations. The initial mission of those organisations providing residential accommodation was to *rescue* children from what were seen as demoralising families or conditions and to save them, both physically, but more importantly spiritually. This distinguished them from the Poor Law authorities who had no duty to *seek out* children only to *receive* them.

Let us follow, briefly, the biography of Thomas Barnardo, as an illustration of some of the major themes of the Victorian philanthropic movement. Barnardo became an evangelical Christian at the age of 17 in 1862. He moved to London in 1866 and was soon moved by the plight of the homeless and rootless children he encountered on the streets. Guided by a young man called Jim he witnessed the situation of many young people abandoned to the evils of the street. In 1870 he established his first home for boys. Following an incident where a young man nicknamed 'Carrots' died when Barnardo's home was full, Barnardo was moved to place a sign on his establishment stating 'NO DESTITUTE CHILD EVER REFUSED ADMISSION'. In 1873 he opened his first home for girls, at the Barkingside site which was to develop into a model of cottage homes for children. Girls, Barnardo felt, produced a particular challenge for his organisation and needed special attention if they were to succeed. The Barnardo ethos was to emphasise training and education to ensure that the children were saved from pauperism. This was organised along lines felt appropriate for each sex – basically manual trades for the boys, and preparation for going into service for the girls. The earlier theme of emigration again emerges in the context of the great Victorian philanthropic organisations. They too felt attracted to the idea of giving children a new start in the colonies. This policy crystallised many ideas and philosophies held by the philanthropists.

First, there was the belief that children needed to be separated from their families. Children were sometimes told that they were orphaned when this was not the case, and information about their parents was deliberately withheld. Cale (1993) argues that the tendency to cut children off from their past was part of the moral reform process, a practice Parker refers to as 'active severance'. In her study of case files of reformatory schools during the latter part of the nineteenth century Cale argues:

> They did not consider it important to give the children a full understanding of what had happened and why. All that was required was the simple belief that the past had been sinful and wrong, and that the future was to be very different. (1993: 209)

The emigration policy was consistent with this way of thinking and perhaps an extreme example of the perceived benefits of separation from the birth family. Certainly Barnardo's went to some lengths, including withholding the truth from children and young people, to ensure that separation occurred.

Second, the emigration policy also reflected imperialist attitudes. It was regarded as positive that British children could be used to cultivate and develop the colonies. Third, we can also see the belief in the benefits of the open space of the countryside as opposed to the evils of the urban environment which had been felt to contribute to the moral fall of parents. As Barnardo commented 'If the children of the slums can be removed from their surroundings early enough, and can be kept sufficiently long under training, heredity counts for little, environment counts for everything' (quoted in Heywood 1978: 53).

By the turn of the century the great philanthropic child welfare organisations were part of the landscape of British child welfare. They existed in a complex relationship with state provision – and certainly neither sector can truly be understood in isolation.

The growth of state welfare: 1908–39

Key themes:
- The passage of the Children Act 1908;
- The consolidation of state responsibility for the child;
- The challenge to the 'less eligibility' principle.

As the Victorian era reached an end and Britain entered the twentieth century, the social conditions were in place for an extension in the role of the state in welfare. The first ten years of the new decade saw the passage of a number of pieces of major legislation which impacted on child welfare in its broadest sense and, more specifically, on provision for separated children. A number of conditions came together which provided the conditions for these reforms.

First, a number of surveys and reports, including the work of Rowntree (*Poverty : A Study of Town Life* (1901)) and Charles Booth (*In Darker England and the Way Out* (1890)), pointed to the widespread nature of poverty and suggested that the causes lay outside of individual failure and pathology, thereby beginning to discredit the Poor Law. This, along with the findings of the Royal Commission on the Poor Law, particularly the Minority Report which in the long run was more influential than the majority report, lay the basis for a series of major reforms in social welfare.

Second, there was major concern about the health and physical state of British children, and in particular, the fitness of British youth as they entered the Army to fight in the Boer War. This imperialist momentum added some urgency to the reform programme. The Report of the Inter-Departmental Committee on Physical Deterioration, which was published in 1904, provided the empirical data needed to inform child welfare reforms.

Finally, the growth of socialism and organised socialist parties led to social policy reform being seen as a possible method of limiting the growth of socialist thought amongst the population.

These three factors therefore came together to provide the springboard for a major period of social reform. In relation to children, in a period of only two years we saw the introduction of, in 1906, the Education (Provision of Meals) Act and the Education (Administrative Provisions) Act – which introduced school medicals, and in 1908, the Punishment of Incest Act and the Children Act.

In this context we will focus on the later Act, which is sometimes referred to as the 'Children's Charter'. The Children Act of 1908 was primarily a consolidating act, but nevertheless, in bringing together a wide range of child welfare legislation it has been taken by some analysts to symbolise a significant breakthrough in the care of children. Certainly the Act was comprehensive, and can be seen as part of the series of welfare legislation introduced between 1906 and 1908. Heywood states that the Act brought together:

> 19 statutes which contained the law relating to reformatory and industrial schools were consolidated and the Secretary of State given powers to transfer youthful offenders from reformatory to industrial schools thus enabling the largely artificial distinction between them to be broken down, managers of such schools were enabled to board out children sent to them under the age of 8. (Heywood 1978: 108–9)

Further, as far as residential care was concerned, imprisonment for young people under the age of 16 was abolished, and as a consequence, remand homes were established using central government funding. The Act also introduced the inspection of small voluntary homes.

Meanwhile the Royal Commission on the Poor Law had been established in 1905 and was to report in 1909. The famous Minority Report helped to challenge the philosophy of the Poor Law by stating that the Board of Guardians had failed largely because they were 'destitution authorities', that is, they had focused on less eligibility and pauperism. The Minority Report was effectively implemented by administrative rather than legislative means and helped contribute to the provision of more specialised social services, a shift away from less eligibility towards more service-oriented provision. The administrative revolution was led by the Local Government Board, which took over central responsibility for the Poor Law. The board led a shift to ensure that children were no longer accommodated in the workhouse. Boarding out was actively encouraged and the Board recommended that all areas should establish special Children's Committees. The First World War also contributed to a climate where people were felt to have a positive claim on services, rather than provision being seen as something which should be deterred. In 1918 the Local Government Board became part of the Ministry of Health, which became the central government department responsible for the Poor Law.

During the 1920s there was a growing focus on the young offender. Optimism grew about the possibility of reforming the offender and in turn there was a decrease in the use of custodial solutions. The most difficult young people were sent to Home Office Approved Schools. Whilst in theory the industrial and reformatory schools still existed for the poor offender child, this distinction increasingly broke down.

The 1929 Local Government Act abolished the Boards of Guardians and their duties were transferred to the counties and county boroughs. The 1930 Poor Law Act established the Public Assistance Committees to administer the Poor Law. The most momentous Act of the period however was the passage in 1933 of the Children and Young Person's Act. The Act linked neglect of children and young people with offending and brought together the treatment of all children. The Act also distanced the care of children from the Poor Law. This break with the Poor Law and the 'less eligibility' principle was reflected in the provision that 'the Court shall have regard to the welfare of the child'. The Act abolished the distinction between the reformatory and industrial schools, which we have already noted was beginning to dissolve anyway; all these schools were to become Approved Schools. Authorities were given a duty to board children out. The Act also established remand homes, where young people could be remanded in order to ensure that they reappeared at court, where they had committed a serious offence, where the court required more information or to allow the young person to reflect. The Act also tightened up the inspection of voluntary homes. Heywood sums up the impact of the Act – perhaps somewhat optimistically – by stating that, 'the welfare of the child, and not the judgement of society, was now paramount.' If this was the case then 'care' would now be privileged over 'control'. Whilst there may have been some shift in this direction the 'control' element was still much in evidence and children and young people were still subject to harsh, institutional regimes.

The final break with the Poor Law: 1945–1980

Key themes:
* The final break with the Poor Law;
* The increasing emphasis on foster care;
* Developing a specialised role for residential care.

The Second World War was to have a major impact on residential child care. The disruption of the war meant that thousands of children spent periods in public care. The war also created an environment ripe for social reform. The catalyst for reform in the area was a letter sent to *The Times* by Lady Allen of Hurtwood, which drew public attention to the state of public care for children and young people. Lady Hurtwood published further observations in her pamphlet 'Whose Children?'. In response to the resulting pressure the government established the Curtis Committee:

> …to inquire into the existing methods of providing for children who from loss of parents or from any cause whatever are deprived of a normal home life with their own parents or relatives; and to consider what further measures should be taken to ensure that these children are brought up under conditions best calculated to compensate them for lack of parental care. (Heywood 1978: 143)

A similar committee under the stewardship of a Mr J.L. Clyde was established in Scotland. The two committees, whilst having slightly different briefs, made very similar recommendations. Their major criticism was of the fragmented and unco-ordinated method of caring for children, therefore suggesting the establishment of a unified system for administering child care at local government level. There should be chief Children's Officers who were responsible to local Children's Committees. They also made recommendations to improve training, reception centres to assess the needs of children and the importance of after-care. Significantly for residential child care, Curtis proposed the adoption of the family group home model: small mixed homes of around eight boys and girls, cared for by consistent care figures.

These findings were to be largely enacted in the Children Act of 1948, which together with the National Insurance Act of 1946 and the National Assistance Act of 1948, represented, in the post-Beveridge climate, a clear break with the Poor Law. The 1948 Children Act finally established a legal basis on which high quality residential child care could be delivered. Section 12(1) of the Act stated that: 'Where a child is in the care of a local authority it shall be the duty of that authority to exercise their powers with respect to him so as to further his best interests, and to afford him opportunity for the proper development of his character and abilities.' The reception centres, suggested by Curtis, introduced a duty to receive children and young people into care on a voluntary basis, and emphasised that the religious needs of the child must be met and placed stronger after-care duties on the authorities. The Act also placed a duty on the local authorities to restore the child to the family wherever possible – breaking with the child rescue ideology of the Victorian era.

The 1948 Act was to establish the climate in which residential care was to develop during the 1950s and 1960s. Residential care developed around three key institutions – the reception or assessment centre, the family group home and the Approved School.

The reception centres acted as a first port of call for children in care on a voluntary or statutory basis. They functioned according to a set of ideas influenced by developmental psychology, where the needs of the child could be measured and assessed. In theory the centres established the needs and this assessment was used as the basis for the future placement of the child. The family group home became the main unit for the long-term placement of children and young people. As suggested by Curtis these were small homes, often 'ordinary'-looking houses, perhaps on council estates and often managed by a married couple who worked as housemother and housefather. The home then was designed to reflect the family as far as possible. Offenders were sent to the Approved School, usually large residential schools in rural settings. The regime in these homes was more rigid and disciplinarian than in the family group homes.

The primary development of the period, however, was the challenge to the residential institution which came from the research of John Bowlby. Bowlby's theory of maternal deprivation was highly influential. His study, published in 1953, examined children based in isolation wards and argued that disturbed or delinquent behaviour by children and young people was the result of lack of consistent and adequate mothering during their early years. This research was consistent with the preference of the Curtis Committee and the 1948 Act for fostering, and also coincided with the concern of the social democratic consensus to break with the Poor Law, which was symbolised by institutionalised forms of care. Research by Bowlby and others could be used to back the argument that fostering should be privileged over residential care. As Packman argues:

> Publication at a time when Britain had just framed new legislation for deprived children gave [Bowlby] both a ready made audience and an administrative structure within which his theories could be put into practice and tested further. Few research studies can have had such a favourable launching, nor such a profound impact. (Packman 1981: 23)

The impact of this research was then to help establish a clear hierarchy of child placement – adoption, fostering and, least desirable, residential care. The proportion of children in care who were fostered increased from 29 per cent in 1946, to 37 per cent in 1950 to about half of all young people in care by the end of the 1950s.

The other trend of the period was the development of preventive work with families, using casework skills to prevent the need for children and young people to enter the care system. This direction was reinforced by the Ingelby Committee which reported in 1960, and whose concern with prevention was enshrined in Section 1 of the 1963 Children and Young Persons Act. The Ingelby Committee also furthered the trend of bringing together responses to both delinquent and deprived children and young people.

The impact of these two trends – the development of preventive work, alongside the growth of fostering, particularly of younger children – meant that residential care became increasingly provision for older young people, young people with disabilities and those considered to have severe problems which made them unsuitable for fostering.

Meanwhile the trend towards seeing neglected children as having shared problems with those children and young people who had been involved in offending reached a high point with the passage of the 1969 Children and Young Persons Act. In 1968 the Labour government introduced a White Paper, *Children in Trouble* (Home Office 1969). The content of the White Paper was very much led by two key civil servants, Joan Cooper and Derek Morrell. Their proposals reflected their belief in promoting the welfare of the young person and to the conflation of the 'delinquent' and 'deprived' categories of children and young people. This White Paper formed the basis of the 1969 Act. The main points of the Act have been summarised elsewhere (Frost and Stein 1989: 81) as:

(a) raising the age of criminal responsibility from 10 to 14 years old
(b) using care proceedings for 16- and 17-year-olds whenever possible
(c) treatment being voluntarily agreed between social workers and parents without a court appearance, wherever possible
(d) mandatory police consultation with social services before prosecuting 14- to 17-year-olds
(e) replacing detention centres and attendance centres by schemes of intermediate treatment
(f) care orders to replace Approved School and Fit Persons Orders
(g) the minimum age for Borstal training to be raised from 15 to 17 years of age.

The Act was in many ways the high point of the welfare approach to working with children and young people. However, before the Act could be implemented, a retreat from this position had begun, largely due to the election of a Conservative government in 1970. We witnessed a retreat from welfare to a justice model (see Frost and Stein 1989: 82–86).

What impact did these developments have on residential child care? It is apparent that residential child care did not decline following the 1948 Act, in the way suggested by the preference of both that Act and the Curtis Committee for fostering. In 1955 there were 21,941 young people in local authority residential care; by 1972 this figure had remained remarkably similar at 20,548. Far from declining and being seen as a residual and outdated service, Packman argues that by the mid-1970s residential child care came to be 'regarded as both an important and integral part of the service and it covers a wide range of establishments of different size and specialism' (1981: 147).

Following the Children and Young Persons Act 1969, the development of diversion and alternatives to custody and schemes led to a reduction of the number of young people placed in Community Homes with Education (CHEs).

It was in the 1980s that we saw a more rapid decline in the use of residential child care. In 1980 there were approximately 17,000 children in various types of local authority homes, a figure which declined to under 15,000 in 1985 and to under 8,000 by 1990. What factors were at play during the 1980s?

First of all there was the impact of the permanence movement. Rowe and Lambert (1973) found many children in residential care drifting without firm plans being made for their futures. This research had a considerable impact, leading to stronger plans for children being put in place, many of which emphasised the importance of a quick return home and, failing this, adoption or long-term fostering. Again, rather like the impact of the Bowlby research, residential care was challenged and policies tended to work against it.

Second, the anti-institutional thinking of the 1960s (Goffman 1961) continued to have an impact, so that fieldworkers and those (largely ex-fieldworkers) who became managers in social services departments often carried with them ideologies which were wary of the impact of institutions on children and young people.

Third, the economics and ideology of foster care continued to be attractive to the new social services departments of the 1970s, which were to become the financially limited departments of the 1980s.

These factors and perhaps others all came together to contribute to the decline of residential child care during the 1960s and 1970s. In fact, given these factors what is remarkable is the resilience of the residential sector and the fact that social services departments recognised that they could not survive without residential provision for children (the exception being Warwickshire, see Cliffe and Berridge, 1991).

We therefore leave this brief historical survey at a low point for residential child care. This history is picked up in Chapter 4, on the Children Act, in

Chapter 7, and on the abuses and uses of residential child care. We argue that two key events helped to make developments in residential care more positive and optimistic. These two key events were first, somewhat paradoxically, the response to the 'scandals' in residential care in the late 1980s, and second, the passage of the 1989 Children Act itself.

Conclusion

In this chapter we have seen how residential child care has developed historically and socially. Weaving throughout the historical facts and dates are a number of key themes:

- The operation of care cannot be separated from the exercise of power. The power to separate children from their families, to send the children abroad and to regulate them within care settings. This makes the care system intrinsically political – a site where the exercise and distribution of power is contested.
- The care system always bears a relationship to wider social and political themes – we cannot understand the care system without relating it to issues of social class, gender, disability and ethnicity, for example.
- Because of the issues of power and politics there is within the care system a tension between 'control', 'care' and 'resistance'. All these three themes are present within any care setting – the way that this tension is played out, however, will vary and be unique to each care setting.

In the next chapter we will return to these themes, using social theory to assess whether further light can be cast on these issues.

2   Theoretical approaches to residential child care

Introduction

In this chapter we examine a number of theoretical approaches to residential care. The aims of the chapter are to examine a range of prominent theoretical frameworks, and to develop a contemporary theoretical framework which will inform the empowering practice which we wish to promote.

The relationship between theory and practice is a difficult and controversial one. In terms of residential care we can perhaps detect two levels of theory in play – we can identify these as macro, or grand, theories which attempt to provide overarching explanatory frameworks, and micro, often behavourial, theories which claim a direct relevance to direct practice with children and young people. In this chapter we draw on the macro theories: if these are adequately conceptualised and reformed they can be utilised to provide overall, contextualising theory and to inform micro-practice (an issue we examine in Chapter 3 on empowering young people).

In this section we aim to examine three theoretical approaches which might be helpful in informing our empowerment framework. These perspectives are not at all comprehensive – there are numerous other theoretical perspectives. We have selected three key perspectives on the grounds that they all place power at the centre of their analysis. The following theoretical frameworks will be examined in some detail:

- *Interactionist perspectives* – using Erving Goffman as an example of such a perspective
- *Foucauldian perspectives* – examining how the work of Michel Foucault

can be utilised to understand residential child care
* *Social control perspectives* – as an example of a 'critical' perspective.

Each perspective is explored in terms of how it helps to advance our under-standing, and also in terms of the reservations we have about each perspective. The chapter concludes with an examination of a theoretical framework which we will use to inform this study.

Interactionist perspectives

While the American sociologist Erving Goffman has never written directly about residential child care, some aspects of his work are very helpful in helping us think about group care for children and young people. In particular Goffman researched a study, *Asylums*, which examines how institutions work.

The key concept utilised by Goffman that is relevant to us is that of the 'total institution'. Goffman identified total institutions as those institutions which encompass the three key aspects of our life – work, play and sleep. Most of us undertake these activities in different settings – but for residents of total institutions all these activities take place in the same site and under the same form of authority.

Goffman identifies four key features of total institutions:

1   all activities take place in one setting under one authority
2   activities take place in groups or collectivities
3   activities are tightly scheduled
4   activities are brought together in a single rational plan to fulfil the aim of the institution.

He sees these institutions as a 'social hybrid', that is, they combine residential communities with the features of formal organisations. What interests Goffman is that these institutions are, 'forcing houses for changing persons; each is a natural experiment on what can be done to the self' (1961: 22).

Goffman's ideas on asylums may be helpful in getting us to think about group care for children and young people. Do contemporary community homes share any of the features of Goffman's total institution or can we make a clear distinction between total institutions and child care establishments? It may be the case that the 'good' community home might actually be one which displays none of the features described by Goffman.

Let us examine one of Goffman's key ideas in order to fill out our under-standing of theory. Goffman identified the 'degradation ceremony' as a key moment in the total institution. This ceremony takes place at the moment of admission to the institution, a moment which we might also like to reflect is significant in group care for children and young people.

The ceremony takes place when one arrives at an institution. As a new inmate/resident arrives they carry with them the signs and symbols of their own unique identity – clothes, hairstyle, jewelry, etc. In order that the resident can be integrated into the total institution they must be stripped of the signs of this identity. This allows the new inmate to be identified as one who must participate in all the rituals of the institution and also illustrates that the individual is stripped of power – the institution is in charge. This degradation ceremony is an essential process which must take place before the individual can enter the institution.

For Goffman the resident can handle the regime in a number of manners. Initially the resident undergoes a 'primary adjustment' – adjusting their conception of self to respond to the regime. There is also a 'secondary adjustment': this is a method adopted by the individual in order to stand aside from the role that has been assigned for them. Through this the resident 'plays the system', a role that is central to Goffman's sociology.

Residents can also challenge the regime. This idea is similar to that expressed by Foucault, whose ideas we will examine later in this chapter. Foucault argues that where there is power there is also resistance. This resistance can be seen to take place on a continuum – from fairly mundane forms of daily resistance to more overt and politicised forms of resistance. An example of resistance is the use of secret languages by children and young people in residential care. One of the authors has witnessed a unit where the young people developed an entire secret language which had the effect of excluding staff from their interactions. The language consisted of a simple linguistic technique (in this case switching letters in words) but meant that the young people could converse in a way that staff could not understand or respond to. More overt forms of resistance could take the forms of organised 'in care' groups (see Stein 1983).

Goffman's theory has been very significant in helping us understand institutions. This theory coalesced with those of R.D. Laing and anti-psychiatry to create a consensus in the 1960s and 1970s against the asylum and the total institution. They were seen as dehumanising and stigmatising: institutions which themselves created illness and dependency. The critique worked against all forms of residential care and the decline in the number of children's homes of the 1970s and 1980s was partly informed by these sociological critiques.

Goffman's and related theories have been very helpful in pointing out the dehumanising aspects of institutional care. They have helped make us aware that the regimes which for example, depended on collective shoe cleaning and other forms of routinisation, were actually exercises of power and control which helped to depersonalise and create dependency. This theory also helps us understand the 'symbolic' as well as the 'real' function of such activities.

The problem with Goffman's ideas are that they tend to over-emphasise the signs and symbols that no doubt are important. To Goffman it sometimes seems we are made up of masks, of signs and symbols – and that behind these masks for Goffman there seems to be nothing. This is a relativist position: we are what we choose to be and what we wish to present to others (hence the title of another key text of Goffman's *The Presentation of Self in Everyday Life*, 1969). It is hard in this world of symbols to pick out real difference and real inequality – we would argue that poverty, for example, cannot really be understood as a sign, or a mask; it is, rather, a material reality. Walton and Elliot also criticise Goffman on grounds of methodology and for clustering together all institutions as if they were all the same: 'He gives insufficient weight to the varying functions which institutions fulfill, the diverse ways in which they carry out their functions, and fails to recognise that "asylum" in the original sense of the word could still be a valid function' (1980: 7).

We therefore need to learn from Goffman's considerable insights and to use other theoretical insights to build on the valuable contribution which he has made.

Foucauldian perspectives

The work of Foucault represents an intellectual revolution in human thought and has produced work which straddles traditional disciplines – history, philosophy, critical theory, sociology and more. Foucault has focused much of his work on the construction of the social institution – notably the mental hospital and the prison. It is from this work that we may find some indicators which will help us to understand residential child care.

At the centre of Foucault's thought is the idea that social institutions are constructed as part of the exercise of power: even the most private aspects of our life, such as sexuality, are subject to the exercise of power and control. Social institutions are material expressions of the exercise of this power. Foucault's attempts to understand all aspects of institutions in this way – their location, design, architecture – speak to us about the way that power is exercised.

Foucault writes of the prison as the complete institution. He argues that it emerged as a new regime of discipline in modern society, taking over from public torture as the new, 'rational', technique of punishment. This new system of punishment emerged alongside the decline of the feudal system and the dominant role of the sovereign around the beginning of the seventeenth century.

Foucault identifies the following features as defining the prison: hierarchical observation, normalising judgement and the examination. We shall examine each in turn.

Hierarchical observation

Foucault argues that discipline relies on observation as its basic technique. This model reached its ideal type in the Panopticon, designed as a prison by the English utilititarian Jeremy Bentham. The central principle of the design was that it enabled all prisoners to be under continuous observation. Foucault proposes one of his central theses here: that power is a positive force that is present throughout social life and is reflected in the architecture of buildings. For Foucault no building is innocent and certainly in the design of institutions we can detect techniques in the exercise of power. Foucault describes this as: 'an architecture that would operate to transform individuals: to act on those it shelters, to provide a hold on their conduct, to carry the effects of power right to them, to make it possible to know them, to alter them. Stones can make people docile and knowable' (1977a: 172). Power is exercised through the design of these buildings: 'It is power that seems all the less "corporal" in that it is more subtly "physical"' (1977a: 177).

Normalising judgement

The new regime which Foucault examines had at its core the normalising judgement – that is, that all subjects should aspire to a norm of behaviour. In institutions this is dependent on 'a small penal mechanism', which involves punishments, withdrawal of privileges, disapproval and so on. The regime centres on that 'which does not measure up to the rule, that departs from it' (1977a: 178). Punishment in these regimes is corrective in nature, it is aimed at changing something in the individual. All behaviour, Foucault argues, falls on a continuum of good and evil and is evaluated on this basis. The technique of judgement involves assessing actions along this continuum. By assessing acts with precision, discipline judges individuals 'in truth': 'the penality that it implements is integrated into the cycle of knowledge of individuals' (1977a: 178).

Thus the actions of the individuals are assessed against a whole. It locates individuals in comparison with one another and differentiates them through measurable criteria. This in turn establishes a norm to be aspired to, which in turn establishes what should be seen as beyond the norm – the abnormal.

All these techniques establish the 'Norm'. The human sciences of 'psych-' regulate the Norm through the related professions: the psychologists, the psychiatrists, social workers, teachers and so on.

The examination

The aim of the examination, according to Foucault, is to classify, qualify and punish. It is a central ritual through which the action of power is exercised. The examination is about the subject being visible and exposed to normalising judgement – this contrasts with medieval discipline where the subject was invisible (i.e. locked away). The examination crucially 'individualises' the subjects – they are classified and records are kept which identify them as unique individuals with peculiar characteristics: 'All the sciences, analyses or practices employing the root "psycho-" have their origin in...the procedures of individualisation' (1977a: 193).

While Goffman in *Asylums* examines mental hospitals, Foucault (having examined mental institutions in *Madness and Civilisation*) looks at the prison in *Discipline and Punish*. Foucault identifies the following features of the 'complete institution' (in comparison with Goffman's concept of 'total institutions'):

(1)   Prisoners are isolated from the outside world and also from each other, as gatherings are regarded as dangerous. This isolation fits with the individualising practices of the 'psych' human sciences.
(2)   A regime of routine is established, which in prisons is based on work.
(3)   The exercise of a regime exists to reform the incarcerated individuals.

In order to exercise this regime the person becomes identified as a 'delinquent' rather than the 'convict'. The delinquent is identified through the characteristics of their life – not simply through the law-breaking act. It is through the act that one is incarcerated but the regime has permission to act on the life, the whole identified individual. This is where the role of the human sciences is crucial.

Foucault then gives us a new perspective on the institution. Like Goffman, Foucault's work is not specifically about residential child care; however, we can learn from Foucault and transfer some of his ideas to help us understand residential child care in more depth.

The social control critique

The social control critique of residential care is something which has existed in theory and in practice – often centring on the critique of the workhouse and its various ancestors. We are not aware of any single text or representative author who could symbolise this position - thus we draw on a range of authors and perspectives, who we bring together under the loose definition of being left-wing critics of residential provision.

The left critique begins with the formulation that sees social policy as a form of social control. Many on the left have argued that it is naive to see social policy functioning simply as a method of 'caring for people'. For example, the National Health Service would not be seen as simply about making people better – it would be analysed as part of the state's mechanisms which contribute to the process of capitalist production by enabling people to return to work. Thus social welfare policies have been seen as having two main functions: to contribute to the conditions which ensure the successful accumulation of profit, and to create the necessary conditions for social harmony, which allow accumulation to continue unhindered.

Residential child care can be seen to function in this way first of all historically. As we have previously seen early residential provision was closely linked to the Poor Law. The workhouse operated as a form of less eligibility – a principle which was designed to ensure that no one would enter the workhouse unless it was absolutely necessary. People would do all they could to endure conditions on the outside, including working for low wages. Piven and Cloward see this as a clear and explicit function of the workhouse: 'Conditions in the workhouses were intended to ensure that no one with any conceivable alternatives would seek public aid. Nor can there be any doubt of that intent' (1972: 33).

It follows from this that Poor Law regimes had to ensure that conditions were harsh and not attractive to potential residents. This in turn helped to regulate the lifestyles of the mass of the working population, encouraging them to work for low wages in harsh conditions. Historically, the left's analysis argues that the residential establishment exists as a form of social control. As Lee and Pithers point out: 'By the left it [residential care] is regarded as one more agency of punitive control integral to the continuation of the existing bourgeois order' (87: 1980). Offe provides an example of this when he argues that residential establishments exist for controlling those who are 'engaging in deviant, criminal, or other kinds of behaviour that are considered to be incompatible with the orderly pursuit of surplus value production' (Offe, in Senior 1989: 234).

The second function of residential child care – that of creating harmonious social conditions, in which capitalist social relations can reproduce themselves – is carried out by residential child care providing for those who otherwise would be a threat to the social order by being homeless and rootless, evicted from the family home and so on. According to this line of debate, capitalist democracies 'care' for their populations so that the general population acquiesces to the existing social system.

The left critique would also extend to the functioning of residential institutions. Here the argument would run that as apparatuses of the capitalist state social institutions reproduce hierarchical social conditions within them. Homes are thus run as hierarchies, which promote dominant social relations and ideas. An historical example would be the homes of Barnardo that we have already mentioned. The homes actively promoted religion, which in terms of the left critique would be part of the social cement. They also, for example, reproduced dominant gender relations by stereotyping male and female roles through job training and apprenticeships for industrial roles and domestic work roles. There is also a trend in the left critique which, as Cohen says, contrasts 'between the good community – open, benevolent, accepting – and the bad institution – damaging, rejecting, stigmatizing' (1985: 185), which shares much in common with the Goffman perspective which we have already examined.

The left critique is essentially political and therefore proposes a political practice in relation to residential care. Senior (1989) and Lee and Pithers (1980) challenge the left orthodoxy by arguing that a progressive political practice is possible in residential care: 'We believe residential child care can transcend the limitations we have attributed to the liberal-therapists and be developed as a vital crucible for testing the political possibilities of alternative forms of care' (Lee and Pithers 1980: 109).

This optimism is largely rooted in the position, which would be shared by some feminists, that residential care can represent a challenge to the family, which can be seen as one of the primary institutions which promote the reproduction of capitalist social relations. Lee and Pithers quote a Camden local authority policy document which establishes their main points:

challenge competition and individualism
to develop group awareness and interdependence
to build up self-confidence and interdependence of each child so that they can fully participate in the group
to break down hierarchies
to challenge the domination of the weak by the strong
to break down stereotyped sex roles
to develop warm emotional relationships not exclusive to the nuclear family
to develop an understanding of political questions (Lee and Pithers 1980: 110)

To this list Lee and Pithers would add: 'to combat racism' (1980: 110).

Residential care can be an example of a form of collective living which challenges the hegemony of the family. Equally, residential care can, at least in theory, be organised in a way which challenges authoritarianism and hierarchies by promoting equality and participative democracy. This then can be seen as a form of progressive practice within the institutions of capitalism.

Understanding the whole

Goffman, Foucault and the social control theorists have made a substantial contribution to our awareness of the power of institutions to shape and influence the lives of 'inmates' – through institutionalisation, observation, examination, normalising judgment and 'historical' regulation. They have also made us aware of the other side of the equation: resistance and resilience, and the potential to develop other alternative forms of care. These theorists thus capture the messages from history outlined earlier and provide a foundation for developing a new understanding of residential child care derived from the uses and abuses of power.

Our perspective begins with a recognition of the different ways children who enter residential child care may be dis-empowered:

1 *Familial context* – the experience of physical, emotional and sexual abuse; neglect; family difficulties and behavourial problems.
2 *Substitute familial context* – most young people in residential settings have had unsuccessful foster care placements, usually on more than one occasion. Perhaps not surprisingly in view of this and the familial problems mentioned above, research evidence suggest high levels of emotional and behavioural problems among young people entering residential child care (Berridge and Brodie 1998).
3 *Societal: inequality* – there is a well-established link between social deprivation and entry to care (see Bebbington and Miles 1989). In addition to the familial contexts mentioned above, many young people entering care have lived in poor families and deprived neighbourhoods.
4 *Societal: divisions* – specific groups of young people entering care may have experienced specific issues and problems associated with being black or mixed heritage, disabled or gay, for example.
5 *Societal: generation* – in common with other young people those entering residential child care are subject to the same confused and ambiguous messages given to young people in contemporary society (Jenks 1997). Associated with this are the pressures of consumerism and the complexities faced by young people in what some commentators identify as 'post-modern' society.

A recognition of these five dimensions and their interrelationship gives us a framework for helping to understand why residential child care work can be so difficult and challenging. Children's homes exist because families and society have failed their children and young people. These five dimensions also help us understand that residential managers and staff alone cannot empower children and young people – the task is a much wider one. However, in understanding the nature of this task it remains the case that residential staff can make a significant contribution to empowering children and young people. The subsequent chapters aim to explore how this can be achieved.

Conclusion

In a complex society such as ours, all the social divisions we have mentioned will be at play in a residential establishment – it is important to understand how these factors interact and interrelate. We would argue that a residential situation is a complex whole where the divisions of our social formation are to be found; it is a site where there are struggles over power between staff and young people, and within the groups of young people and staff group. It is for this reason why we think that texts and practices which emphasis either the caring and therapeutic aspects of residential care or the professional approach to care can only grasp part of the picture. A more complex theory needs to address the inequality and power issues we have mentioned.

The complexity of this whole means that residential care cannot be understood either by a crude leftism which focuses on 'social control', or on residential care as a form of state domination. The complexity means that no 'reductionist' theory is adequate – that is we cannot understand residential care simply as 'racist', 'sexist' or which ever oppression we wish to highlight. We need to focus more on the interplay of factors and on the issue of power which, as any residential worker will testify, does not rest simply in the hands of 'the staff'.

Why is the idea of residential child care simply promoting the welfare of the child inadequate? We would argue that residential establishments actually have a more ambivalent role in society – they provide both care and control. The control factor, as we have seen in our historical chapter, has deep roots in the formation of British residential care in the Poor Law and the fear of the poor and vagrant by 'respectable' society. Whilst 'caring' might be the motivation of the individual carer we cannot escape the heavy weight of history.

Equally we need to distinguish between the differential impact of residential care on the different groups of young people we have mentioned. It is not helpful therefore to group all young people together as a single, homogenised group. We must, rather, consider the differential impact of care on different groups of children and young people.

We are proposing a theory of residential child care which problematises the role of residential child care and the differential impact on young people. It is for this reason that power and social division is central to our analysis.

First of all what does it mean to say that the residential unit is a site for the exercise of power? We would agree with Foucault, who, as we have seen, has argued that power is exercised through classificatory mechanisms – the exercise of the 'psych' complex which analyses, classifies and records information on the child and young person. Foucault is, however, reluctant to trace a source of this power – he would find this reductionist. We would argue that this reluctance to track down power leaves us with only a partial analysis. In the context of residential care we have no problem arguing that the location of this power is normally the state, or more usually the local state. We can therefore argue that residential child care is a site for the exercise of forms of state power.

However, we would not wish this argument to allow us to be identified with the social control position which we have already identified. For us, this state power is a complex phenomena: it is de-centred and divided, it is exercised by national and local politicians, by civil servants and local government officers, by professionals with different perspectives and is often challenged and reformed by the actions of the young people themselves. By identifying the state as the source of the power exercised in residential establishments we are certainly not arguing that state power is centralised or uncontested.

Here then we have the base line for a theory of empowerment. It is a theory which is political in the way that it approaches residential child care and which draws on a range of social explanation in order to understand residential child care and to build a coherent approach to practice in residential child care.

3 Empowering children and young people

Introduction

In this chapter we propose that the empowerment of young people in residential care should be the central focus of the residential child care task. It is essential, however, that the exploration of empowerment is first located in an appropriate context in order to avoid empowerment becoming a meaningless slogan.

We will therefore consider the wider social, political and economic climate which influences the lives of children and young people generally in society as young people in residential care do not live in a vacuum. They are both affected by and reactive to the wider social environment in which they live. Staff therefore need to be aware of the wider social context and how this impacts on children and young people whom they look after.

Having established this wider context we will then move on to consider the residential care environment at both the macro and micro levels. We then move on to examine in more detail the relation between empowerment and the more familiar concept of children's rights. This will be followed by an examination of practical strategies for empowering young people particularly in relation to their race, ethnicity, gender, disability and sexuality.

Young people in context

Young people in the United Kingdom today face a fragmented and uncertain future with regard to employment, housing, and economic sustainability as they experience the transition period between the dependency of childhood and the shift to adulthood. Whilst facing the complexities of this transition, young people have to face the demands of the rapidly changing, post-modern world and the pressures of consumption that it brings with it. Bea Campbell expresses some of these tensions as follows: 'All over the peripheral estates across Britain, teenagers were wearing designer casuals that signified their refusal to be peripheral, to be on the edge of everything' (1993: 271).

The complexity of the transition to adulthood gives impetus to the tendency to view young people as problematic. Geoffrey Pearson argues that there is an association between the conceptions of 'youth' and of 'modernity' which tends to problematise youth: '"Youth" is both a signifier of ... unwelcome changes, and their embodiment. The rising generation is not only "new"; it has no option other than to embrace the present and its implied future in whatever terms it is presented, if it is to make its way in the world' (1994: 1194).

These changes are particularly associated with socially deviant behaviour – crime, sexuality and drug use. Thus youth is almost always viewed to be in crisis – there is almost always a 'moral panic' about some aspect of youth.

Young people in residential care feel all the pressures which face contemporary young people in addition to the pressures and stigma arising from separation from their families. We can say in this way that they are carrying a double challenge of being young and of being separated from their family. The pressure of being 'looked after' brings with it fear and stigma. Young people in the care system often talk about being regarded either as 'criminals' or 'orphans'. We know a young person who visits her friend whose mother cannot believe that she is in a 'home' because she is too 'nice'.

Additionally in residential care we have also seen a series of demographic changes which have had a profound impact on the make-up of the population in residential child care. We now have a predominantly older population of young people, many of whom will have experienced a series of placement changes during their 'care careers'. Young people are therefore entering residential care when they are older and with fractured and disrupted lives behind them. Sinclair and Gibbs (forthcoming) summarise their extensive survey of looked after people as follows:

> The young people were described by their social workers as troubled and troublesome. Their family situations were highly disrupted, less than one in six had families where both natural parents were still living together. Their behavior was problematic. Seven out of ten had been excluded from school or frequently truanted, six out of ten had at least some involvement in delinquency, sizeable proportions (four out of ten or more) had been violent to adults, violent to other children, run away from care, run away from their own homes and put themselves

or others at risk through sexual behaviour, and more than a third had attempted to commit suicide or harmed themselves.

As well as an older care population we also have a care population in which boys are over-represented. In 1995 53.5 per cent of young people in care were boys (Department of Health 1995)

It is telling that at the moment no nationally available statistics tell us the ethnic make-up of young people in care. We do know that young people from mixed heritage backgrounds are over-represented in the care system (Rowe et al. 1989) and that young black people may often find themselves in a minority in a given establishment. The challenges of addressing 'race' and ethnicity issues in residential care are therefore very real.

As far as disability is concerned a coherent picture is equally difficult to construct. The Council for Disabled Children estimates that there are, 'at least 46,050 such children in some form of residential school or communal provision' (Kahan 1994: 19). Since the implementation of the Children Act it has become clear that disabled children and young people are 'children in need' in the same way that any such child might be and that it follows from this that provision should be integrated wherever possible. Children with disabilities often receive respite or permanent care in residential establishments – and they have particular needs which have to be met if they are to be effectively empowered. A survey conducted as background for the Warner Report found that 'The over-whelming majority of children, about two-thirds are, (in the opinion of those running the homes) in a home because they have emotional and/or behavioural difficulties which make other placements inappropriate' (HMSO 1992: 18). Whilst this survey is acknowledged by Warner to have limitations it nevertheless helps us to formulate the current picture of the reality of residential care establishments.

Finally, in attempting to build a picture of residential child care we, unsurprisingly, cannot gather statistics on how many young people consider themselves to be gay or lesbian. This issue has a particular invisibility which represents a particular challenge to residential staffs.

In general, we can say that we can build a picture of contemporary residential child care working with older young people, from troubled backgrounds, often with a fractured care experience. These young people are living in peer groups and attempting to find a pathway to adulthood in a complex, challenging and fast-changing world.

In Chapter 6 we examine in detail the experiences of young people who have been abused in residential care settings. These 'scandals' have helped to highlight the reality for groups of young people in residential care. They also help to highlight the very real challenges and complexities facing residential care staff and their managers. How can we meet the needs of young people faced with the double burden which we have already outlined? Clear strategies need to emerge which take into account the context we have outlined in the first part of this chapter and then develop a clear and coherent plan for residential child care, which is owned by the organisation as a whole and effectively communicated and reviewed.

As we saw in Chapter 1 on the history of residential child care, there has always been a tension between 'care' and 'control' in the care system. The task of addressing the dilemmas of the 'care'/'control' tensions and of establishing safe and appropriate boundaries for children and young people has perhaps never been more urgent. Having considered the context in which these issues have to be considered we now move on to examine the detailed setting of residential child care establishments.

Residential child care establishments

In order to be in a position where staff can effectively empower young people the physical aspects of providing suitable accommodation need to be addressed. The location and standard of residential child care establishments convey powerful messages to those who are resident in them and to those who work in them.

Location

Any living arrangement which falls outside the dominant image of 'the family' arouses fear and suspicion. Careful consideration and planning therefore need to go into deciding on the location of residential child care establishments. Of course it is not always possible to plan a newly built establishment and compromises may have to be made.

The location of an establishment needs to reflect the overall purpose of the establishment. So, for example, when a community home aims to provide medium- to long-term care in a small group setting, it will probably make sense for the home to be located in the heart of an identifiable community. It will be important that the building is adequately maintained and that positive links are built with the community.

In planning a new community home forging effective links from the outset will be essential. Providing a forum for the staff to meet immediate neighbours can be a positive first step. It should be possible to share information from the Statement of Purpose, without compromising the confidentiality of individual young people. The simple step of neighbours visiting the home can help to break down some of the preconceptions and prejudices which they may hold. Many people still have images of residential establishments which draw on the practice and ideology of the Poor Law: 'Children's homes are strongly associated in the public mind with deprived and delinquent children. Dickensian images of the 19th century orphanages linger on' (HMSO 1992: 11).

Face-to-face encounters between staff and neighbours can provide a reference for future meetings, which may well be about problematic issues. Neighbours then have a real person, rather than a stereotype, in mind when they wish to approach the establishment in the future. Links with neighbours and other parties in the communication are important in laying an effective community base for the establishment. Creative use of the resources within the staff team need to be constantly addressed. For instance, a member of the team may have a particular contribution to make in the local community which might involve offering to share a particular talent or skill at the local youth club. Not only can this demonstrate a willingness to help, but can also enable the young people to feel proud of where they live and that it is making a positive contribution to the locality.

If particular problems arise in relations with the local community which directly involve the behaviour of some of the young people being seen as problematic it may be productive to facilitate a forum where both sides can be brought together in a meaningful dialogue. Of course this is never easy and careful preparation needs to take place.

Another reality of residential child care is that it sometimes becomes necessary for staff to protect the boundaries of the establishment from potentially negative outside influences. Residential child care establishments are often targets for people whose motivation might be to exploit what they perceive to be vulnerable young people. Such people might range from local young people looking for trouble to more sinister adults who might be involved in drugs or prostitution, for example. Establishment staff need to be aware of the legal requirements of the Children Act which require them to approve any visitors to the home.

A familiar scenario is one where the community home is being regularly used by groups of young people from the locality only to discover that none of the group have particular relationships with the young people who are resident. When properly consulted young people might say that they felt uncomfortable with such arrangements but lacked the confidence to challenge them.

It is here where we feel that the concept of empowerment can be particularly helpful. Staff taking the sort of controlling role we have described above may feel uncomfortable. It could be argued that young people have 'rights' to receive visitors – even if they might be the local pimp or drug pusher! This is not so. Individual rights exist in a tension with collective rights to privacy and security. The perceived individual rights of one young person may be in conflict with those of the group. Equally the 'right' for one young person to receive a particular visitor might be perceived by staff not to be in the long-term interests of the young person, particularly if that person might abuse them or exploit them. An empowerment framework would therefore take a longer-term view than a simple 'rights' framework.

The rights of the young people are therefore more complex than individual claims to particular rights. They need to be considered in the context of group rights, of obligations and responsibilities to the group, and to empowerment, which may or may not enable the young person to exercise their 'rights' in the immediate context. It is how these 'rights' and 'responsibilities' are communicated that is crucial. In our experience young people respond to firm, fair and clear boundaries which are *constantly* negotiated with the young people and *consistently* maintained by the staff group.

By maintaining clear outer boundaries, staff can signal that they value the welfare and well-being of the young people they 'look after'. So, for example, expecting one another's friends to behave respectfully to everyone gives a clear message about the safety and care of all young people in the establishment.

Ensuring that establishments are a respected part of the community also involves the actual physical upkeep of the building. As far as possible the building should blend into the community, including being kept in a reasonable state of repair. Again this will signal to the young people, their families and the locality that the young people are valued. The Warner Report puts it like this: 'The success of a child's placement will be adversely affected if the fabric, decor and furnishings of the building are allowed to deteriorate' (HMSO 1992: 99). Young people also need to be involved in decisions about the decorating, furnishing and upkeep of their home: 'Children should be involved in such matters as environment, much as they would be in a family setting' (HMSO 1992: 99).

The size and mix of the resident group of young people

Attention must be given to the size of the group as well as to the mix of young people 'looked after'. With a predominately older age group of young people the need for sufficient space both physically and emotionally is of particular importance. There is a danger of being too prescriptive in stating actual numbers. Clearly the ideal size of a group is determined by a number of factors including the particular role and function of the home, staffing levels, size of the building and budgetary demands. There are however, particular base-line standards which have been established which help to inform decisions about actual numbers:

- Each young person should have a choice of a single bedroom.

- Communal rooms should be large enough to accommodate everyone who shares the space with ease and relaxation.
- Space to meet in private with visitors outside of bedrooms should also be available.
- There is also a requirement to provide for smokers and non-smokers separately for both young people and staff.
- There should be access to a telephone where young people can make phone calls in private.

Taking the above factors into account and balancing these against the economic realities facing welfare agencies we would suggest a figure of around six young people resident to be a realistic figure within the community home provision.

Equally important is the mix of young people. Attention needs to be given in relation to gender, race, ethnicity, disability and sexuality within an overall framework of anti-oppressive practice. Added to this is the need to give careful consideration to the particular emotional and behavioural issues each individual young person brings.

A crucial factor here is the issue of abuse. Whilst there is greater awareness of the particular issue of placing young people with abusing behaviour alongside those who have been abused, such mixes still continue to happen. This is further complicated by our awareness that very often those who abuse have often been victims of abuse themselves. Such blurring of the issues, however, can be unhelpful. Practitioners need to unpick the issues and give clear messages to senior managers about the particular resources needed in order to respond appropriately to the needs of all young people. With this clarity comes the opportunity to design and shape resources in creative and responsive ways. Greater choice of provision is one of the key findings of recent research, summarised as follows in *Patterns and Outcomes in Child Placement*: 'The potentiality for providing much needed specific and specialist services for particular children is increasingly recognised. So too, is the importance of offering choice about the type of placement they prefer' (HMSO 1991: 18).

Empowerment

Having set the wider context we can now consider the concept of empowerment and how this translates into practice for young people in residential child care settings.

As we have said earlier, issues of control are central to any debate about the empowerment of young people. Control in this context needs to be understood clearly as a means of providing the appropriate boundaries to ensure adequate safety to young people who very often experience their lives as out of their control. Quite simply, if young people do not feel safe, they will not be able to respond positively to strategies that are aimed to empower them.

The passage of the Children Act 1989, coinciding with the scandals in residential care, sharpened our attention on the need to provide child-centred, safe and empowering environments for young 'looked-after' people. Discourse on children's rights took a centre-stage position. While this was welcomed by many of us, it was not immediately clear how to negotiate through some of the inherent tensions that existed. In this context thinking about children's rights would seem to have been muddled. It is therefore important that any discussion about the empowerment of young people 'looked after' in group care settings unpicks the complexities of the issues involved.

In considering our practice we cannot ignore the reality of the need to respond appropriately to issues of control that groups of young people living together present us with. These then must be carefully balanced against the need to create opportunities for meaningful involvement of young people within the life of the residential environment.

Practical ways forward

The starting place must be with the organisation as a whole. There needs to be a clear corporate view of the overall provision which should incorporate the principles of the Children Act in seeing residential child care as a positive choice. The organisation also has to give the lead on establishing positive anti-oppressive policies which effectively translate into practice. Responsibility and accountability should be owned by the organisation as a whole for ensuring that a quality service embraces a framework of anti-oppressive practice, thereby enabling it to be an accessible quality service (Simms 1995).

Efforts should be made within residential establishments to ensure that the staff team needs to reflect diversity. Together the team need to work out a shared value base, informed by the principles of anti-oppressive practice, which underpins all their work. The staff team need to feel empowered in order that they themselves can empower young people. The process of involvement is the same for staff and young people and a sense of ownership can only be achieved by involving everyone in the process. The value base will create, alongside the messages conveyed by the physical environment, a culture through which everyone feels valued.

The policies and procedures of the organisation, informed by legislation and research, have to be translated into the life of the establishment. Again the staff team must first understand and assimilate these into a coherent form, open to necessary changes, which can then be shared and adapted with the young people in ways that encourage their participation and ownership of them. There are a number of resources which address particular aspects of policy and practice in residential child care. Time to develop policies and practice is limited within most organisations at operational level – it is therefore important for training sections to resource staff teams with the necessary information and support to assist in this process.

All young people in residential care share a common experience of being 'outsiders' within a society where 'the family' is central. For particular groups of young people, this oppression is supplemented. Research into outcomes for young people in residential care (see Biehal et al. 1995, for example) has highlighted the importance of identity in affecting positive outcomes. Young people with high self-esteem are more likely to survive a poor service delivery: helping young people build a positive identity is crucial therefore to the residential task. There is a particular need to address this for young people in relation to their gender, ethnicity, sexuality and disability. We will now move on to consider these in more detail. For the purpose of clarity we have separated these into categories; however, it is important to remember that the experience of oppression is a holistic experience and might involve aspects of various disadvantages.

Gender

As we said earlier more boys are accommodated in residential care than girls. Within society as a whole, however there are as many girls experiencing the harsh realities that bring young people into a situation where they are 'looked after'. This begs the question of why there are more boys in the system. The answer would seem to lie within the gendered nature of society. Boys are more likely to externalise their behaviour, whereas girls are more likely to internalise. Action equates with the experience for boys: passivity for girls.

In a situation where a boy is experiencing trauma, for whatever reason, he is more likely to demonstrate this to the outside world. His behaviour will be noticed, if only because it presents a problem in school, in the neighbourhood, or at home. For a girl, however, her response to trauma is more likely to be taken inward. She may become withdrawn, may miss school or stay away from the possible trouble spots. In short her behaviour is less likely to be noticed: '... the difference between what women and men do with their *troubles* and with their anger shapes their strategies of survival and solidarity on the one hand, danger and destruction on the other' (Campbell 1993: 303).

If our residential environments generally accommodate more boys the possibility for further abuse or neglect of girls is an issue which cannot be ignored. The rights of one group over another can not go unchecked.

Single-sex environments

Consideration of providing a choice of single-sex environments is one strategy which can be carried forward. Eleven per cent of young people were accommodated in single-sex environments in 1990, with only a third of local authorities providing the choice of this provision: 'It is important to ensure sufficient single-sex homes for those who need them, especially girls who have been sexually abused' (HMSO 1992: 18). The choice of single-sex environments must be provided, however, within a clear framework of positively addressing gender issues, especially in relation to single-sex provision for boys. We are all aware of unhealthy male environments where the worst excesses of male macho behaviour are allowed to thrive.

Mixed-sex environments

Within the mixed-sex provision there is also a need to develop tangible practice which positively addresses the issues for both sexes. Within the physical environment what messages are being conveyed by the pictures on the walls? The books on the shelves? The videos and television programmes watched? Within the staff team what messages are given by the way male and female staff relate to their own and opposite gender? What roles do they each perform? What language do they use? How is humour used? How is one's physicality expressed? How are emotions expressed? How do male staff relate to girls and boys? How do female staff relate to each gender? In short what kind of role models are the staff team providing to the young people and to one another? What is the ratio of girls to boys and what message does this convey? If boys are constantly in the majority due to the demographics mentioned earlier how are these to be positively managed?

   In asking these questions we are not suggesting that answers are easy. They are not. What they do provide is the opportunity to open up discussion within the organisation and amongst the staff team, which will be part of an ongoing process. Issues of power must be constantly addressed as part of the life of the establishment and it is the responsibility of the manager to take the lead on this and to do this in ways which are empowering to all.

Single-sex groups/meetings

There could be occasions when single-sex meetings or groups are run which cover particular issues and topics. For instance, sex education work is usually more effective within single-sex groups. These provide the opportunity to explore issues more deeply within the relative safety of same gender. We would suggest that the girl's group would need to be facilitated by female staff only, whereas the boys may benefit by having both male and female staff involved.

Play and activities

What are the gendered nature of the activities and resources for play that are being provided? Are girls and boys being encouraged to break down the stereotype of what is expected of them? Are girls been encouraged to take part in the more exciting, adventurous pursuits that are stereotypically male? Equally are boys being encouraged to engage in the typically female pursuits? What is the relationship of male and female staff to the activities of the establishment?

Living and sleeping space

How do girls and boys negotiate their space within the building? Who has priority of space? How are bedrooms allocated in relation to gender issues? For instance are boys and girls sleeping next door to one another and having to use bathrooms where in the middle of the night they may bump into one another in a state of sleepy undress? Is it acceptable for young men and women to socialise in one another's bedrooms?

Relationships

What are the nature of the relationships between young men and women? Is it acceptable for sexual relationships between anyone within the home to take place? Within this we include relationships between staff. We would strongly recommend that sexual relationships are not acceptable between anyone involved in the life of the home. Such relationships increase the potential for abuse. A culture can emerge whereby a new girl is pressurised into having sex in order to be accepted by the group. We are also aware of situations of physical abuse by boys on girls who they feel they should have control over. How does this situation empower the young woman in particular, but also the boy himself and the group as a whole? Again taking these kind of decisions can feel contrary to the principle of children's rights but they have a clear rationale based on an understanding of the gendered nature of society that operates in favour of males. In order to create safety for everyone the power imbalances must be responded to in pro-active ways, consistent with anti-oppressive practice.

Staff act as important role models by the way in which they set and keep the appropriate boundaries, both between themselves and with and between young people. When asked by young people why they cannot have a boyfriend or girlfriend within the residential unit we have found them responsive to the view that it is not appropriate or safe to have a relationship with someone you live with at this age and in this context. Young people also respond to fairness and consistency and therefore will appreciate that the boundary also applies to staff. Issues of safety are ones to which again we have found young people to be very responsive. This is particularly so when they have experienced living situations which are unsafe. Setting this kind of boundary names an issue which can easily remain hidden within group living situations. Continuous open discussion on this subject is important to encourage and for staff to engage in with young people.

What we have included in the section specifically on gender also applies to same-sex relationships for the same reasons of inappropriateness and safety.

Race, ethnicity, culture and religion

As we said earlier there are no national statistics referring to the ethnicity of young people in residential care but what we do know is that young black people in many establishments will be in the minority. It is also becoming clearer that children and young people from mixed-heritage backgrounds are more likely to be over-represented within the looked-after system (Rowe et al. 1989).

We also need to be aware of the experience of young people from a wide range of backgrounds which reflects the diverse nature of contemporary society. What are the particular experiences of young people of Irish descent or from the Jewish community or the travelling communities? The need to address issues of empowerment for minority groups within residential child care is of central importance to not only those in the minority but for the group as a whole.

Whether a particular establishment has any black young people resident or not, the staff team should be represented by black workers. Indeed teams should reflect as much diversity as is reasonably and meaningfully possible.

The presence of black workers alone will not create a positive, empowering environment for black or indeed white young people. Clear anti-racist policies and strategies need to be worked out by the team as a whole. Young people will take their cue from staff on how to relate to difference. How are white workers relating to their black and white colleagues? How are white workers relating to black and white young people? How are black workers relating to black and white colleagues and young people? Are the anti-racist strategies being carried out consistently by the whole team?

In our experience young people have responded to such strategies in positive ways. For instance, a white young person rejected a black worker engaged in individual outreach work. The same young person, however, accepted the same worker within a residential setting she was later placed in. Within this context not only were clear messages given consistently about acceptable, anti-racist behaviour and language but also the young person experienced the positive working relationships between all colleagues.

Any policy must be monitored and actioned when necessary if it is to have meaning. It is the responsibility of the manager to ensure that anti-racist policies are adhered to. This is a responsibility that should be passed on in such a way as to involve staff and young people and encourages ownership of the value base. Anti-racist training is an important aspect of this which should be both specific and integrated into all staff training.

As with gender the question of choice of an all-black environment needs to be raised. The numbers involved for some local authorities will be too small for local provision to be a choice but the question needs to be raised and addressed nevertheless. Opportunities for young black people to meet together on their own, facilitated by black workers, should be considered as providing a positive and empowering forum whereby issues of race and ethnicity can be addressed in a pro-active way. Support for this needs to be given throughout the organisation. Where numbers are low, authority or even regionally wide, provision would need to be sought. This can also bring black workers together to co-work.

As with gender, questions about the messages conveyed by pictures, books, videos and television programmes need to be asked and discussed.

What particular attention is being given to religious and cultural expression? How are specific needs around diet and health care being met? Within predominantly white, Christian, English environments what opportunities are being created to bring in other influences as a positive strategy? For black young people who have no contact with black culture, what opportunities for contact are being provided? Are staff and young people aware of organisations that support and advise black young people? Where English is not the first language how are the particular language needs being met?

If positive environments are created which address the needs of black young people there are opportunities for all to broaden their experience in relation to food, culture, music, books, films, stories and more. This may seem somewhat idealistic but we have experience within a residential environment which was far from ideal in many of the aspects already discussed but in relation to anti-racist strategies had a consistent approach that had a positive effect. This example also highlights the need for consistency across all minority groups, and the linking together of the common experience of oppression.

Before considering particular issues relating to disabled young people and lesbian and gay young people, it is worth noting that neither of these groups receives protection in law. Their potential vulnerability is therefore further increased. Awareness of and training in the issues facing these particular groups is generally less available. It is therefore vitally important for staff to have access to training which addresses the issues specific to these groups. The danger with an umbrella approach to anti-oppressive practice is that staff remain unaware of the particular issues facing certain groups. Disablism and heterosexism can result out of simple ignorance of appropriate language, let alone the more complex aspects of oppression.

Disabled young people

The Children Act 1989 refers to disabled children as 'children first'. This emphasis is problematic in its potential to deny or weaken the identity of the disabled child or young person. There is a certain resonance here with the now ill considered view that black children should be considered the same as white children. Being disabled is at the very core of a person's identity and for this not to be acknowledged or to be placed secondary is in itself oppressive. Difference cannot and should not be ignored.

It is important that consideration of disabled young people in residential care is located within a framework which understands that disabled people are disabled by society, and not by their medical condition. Accessibility is therefore the key. And disabled people provide the answers on how to achieve maximum accessibility. This view of course demands that non-disabled people take on board the view that disabled people can and should have control of their lives.

For disabled children and young people their journey through the dual oppression of childhood and disability can be particularly hazardous. It would seem that one of the particular negative consequences of disablism is to view disabled people as permanently in childhood. Thus the transitory period of childhood which signals the end of generational power is not always available to disabled people. The disability rights movement, led and steered by disabled people, has gained momentum over the last few years, and it is crucial that these groups are accessed.

The scandals in residential care form together a devastating catalogue of abuse. For disabled children and young people the potential for abuse is massively increased. The pattern of abuse follows the same categories that Chapter 7 explores – sanctioned, institutional, systematic and individual. In each of these categories the potential for abuse to take place is increased both by disablist attitudes and the level of vulnerabilty disabled children and young people are placed in *vis-à-vis* their carers. These are further compounded if oral English is not the first language.

Within residential child care environments providing respite or permanent care to disabled children and young people, there are particular questions to pose which require detailed attention. How accessible is the building? Whose needs are being served? Are buildings purposely designed to control the movement of the young people? How are drugs used and administered? What are the main reasons for medication? Is medication part of the control aspect?

Are disabled staff employed? If so how do non-disabled staff relate to their disabled colleagues and one another? How are disablist attitudes and humour responded to? How is physical care given? What involvement do young people have in the decisions concerning their care? Does the staff team have the skills to communicate to young people who do not use oral English? What images, books, videos, toys, games are available? What messages do these convey? What opportunities are there for contact and involvement with disabled adults who have a positive identity? What contact is there with support groups, pressure groups, and so on?

Within residential child care environments for 'looked-after' young people, the Children Act is very clear on the need for these to be accessible for disabled young people who may need them. It is important, whether or not disabled young people access the resource, that these environments *are* accessible. This accessibility should include a positive portrayal of disabled people, one which challenges the stereotypical images of dependence and inability. In order for staff and young people to be aware of the particular issues for disabled people, training and access to the necessary resources must be available.

The fundamental need to embrace the philosophy of empowerment through participation and involvement is the same for all young people. As we stressed earlier, in order for staff to embrace this for disabled young people they must first have the awareness and understanding of the issues involved. For most non-disabled staff this involves challenging lifelong assumptions held about disabled people. We have to unpick oppressive attitudes which view disabled people as 'pitiful', 'dependent', 'pathetic' and/or 'fearful'. We also have to face our own uncomfortableness about physical differences. In so doing, however, residential child care environments can be further enriched and strengthened for everyone involved in them.

Lesbian and gay sexuality

Invisibility is at the very heart of any discussion about lesbian and gay sexuality. 'I hid everything that was real to me. I watched the way I walked, the way I talked, the way I smoked a cigarette. No one really knew who I was' (Mallon 1996). Statistics are therefore impossible to access. This invisibility is created out of the homophobic fear, ignorance and mythology that pervades society in relation to lesbian and gay sexuality. Heterosexism operates in two main ways: first in the presumption that everyone is heterosexual which therefore leaves little space for people to express an alternative sexuality, and second, that hetereosexuality is both the 'norm' and the superior lifestyle. Institutional mechanisms serve to keep this status quo. We therefore have psychological and sociological theories which pathologise and categorise lesbian and gay men as 'deviant', as well as a legislative system which operates in ways that criminalises gay men in particular and disadvantages both lesbians and gay men in the civil courts (Logan et al. 1996). Little wonder then that the majority of staff and young people who are lesbian or gay remain invisible. Creating safe environments for lesbian and gay staff and young people to be open about their sexuality is therefore a key task for the organisation as a whole. If the wider organisation embraces this task it will help to create a positive climate within which individual residential environ-ments can build upon.

Youth is a time of intense exploration of identity and a positive identity is at the heart of successful outcomes for looked after young people. The Children Act Guidance does provide a mandate for positive, visible work with young lesbians and gay young men: 'Gay young men and women may require sympathetic carers to enable them to accept their sexuality and develop their own self-esteem' (HMSO 1991: 107).

A very real tension for young gay men, and staff caring for them, is the age of consent being 18. Not only is this discrepant to the heterosexual age of con-sent but it operates within a homophobic climate. Hence the fear of prosecution for a young gay man under 18 is a reality that his heterosexual peers rarely have to face. Staff managing this tension need clear, supportive guidance from the organisation on how to balance the need to give positive and supportive messages to young lesbian and gay people whilst at the same time not be in breach of the law. This is especially necessary since protection in law is not available to lesbian and gay people. There is therefore a danger that the organisation will avoid this by providing training in anti-oppressive practice which fails to name the lesbian and gay experience. Equal Opportunity policies need to explicitly include the wording 'lesbian and gay', rather than the ambiguous 'sexuality', which actually offers little or no protection to lesbians and gay men (Logan et al. 1996). Child care policies also need to give clear messages of support that help and encourage staff to address the issues positively with all young people. Individual establishments will then be in a much stronger position to develop their own internal policies which provide the necessary framework from which tangible work on sexuality can flow.

As with previous sections in this chapter, in addressing the needs of par-ticular groups of young people, we need to be mindful of the messages that the living environment conveys. Is heterosexuality assumed for all and is this message evident in the lack of attention being paid to displaying lesbian and gay images? What books and videos are available? Are these representing lesbian and gay lifestyles? How are homophobic jokes and statements handled? Within sex education discussion is attention being paid to lesbian and gay sexuality? Is gay sexuality only mentioned in relation to HIV/AIDS? How safe is the environment for lesbian and gay staff and young people to be open about their sexuality? There is no conclusive or prescriptive answer about the appropriateness of lesbian and gay staff to be visible to young people. It is the subject of much debate (Logan et al. 1996). But discussion must take place within consideration of all the points already made here and also within the context of appropriate boundaries between staff and young people. We would also pose the question to heterosexual staff about the appropriateness of sharing personal, intimate information. What is important, however, is whether lesbian and gay staff feel safe enough to be open within the staff team. If they do not then this raises serious questions about the team's functioning. If staff do not feel safe then imagine how unsafe a young lesbian or gay person feels within their living environment and the detrimental effects this has on his or her identity.

Lesbian and gay staff are not necessarily best placed to do the direct work with individual or indeed groups of young people on sexuality. The extent to which homophobia pervades may indeed make it very unsafe for lesbian and gay staff to be directly involved. What is necessary is that young people whether or not they are lesbian and gay need clear supportive messages that reinforce a positive lesbian and gay identity. Staff need to be aware of, and give young people access to, support groups and organisations that support and advocate for lesbian and gay young people.

Procedures in residential care

Having considered some of the issues for particular groups of young people we now want to give attention to some of the fundamental processes that are at the core of residential life for all young people. We will begin by addressing the admission procedure.

Admissions

Practitioners are all too aware of the detrimental effects of an unplanned admission into a residential environment that is not organised to receive such admissions. The effects on the individual young person and the group as a whole is even more hazardous. The anxieties of both staff and young people in these circumstances can seriously affect the whole environment. Such decisions to place a young person in an unplanned way are reached by managers who are removed from the real impact of that decision. Very often they will not have met the young person concerned or indeed the group as a whole. When these circumstances arise they are extremely disempowering to everyone. Corporate planning and shaping of residential services within the overall spectrum of services to children and families can help reduce the need for, or at least the impact of unplanned admissions. This approach needs to be at the very heart of the organisation. Within a corporately planned approach the potential for creative, effective and empowering strategies is greatly enhanced. It is to this that we now wish to give attention.

Pre-admission

Prior to the young person arriving into their new living environment it is important to use this time to prepare everyone for the impending admission. In this section we will concentrate on the preparation work from the young peoples' perspective. It is worth remembering that staff will also carry anxiety about the new admission and this needs to be addressed within team and individual supervision settings. Pro-active strategies do of course help to ease everyone's anxiety levels.

Preparation of the group

Young people need to be kept informed about a pending admission. This helps address the particular concerns of the young people which in turn helps them to be more open to a new person joining their group. The information given needs to arrive ideally before the informal networks that young people move in within the care system. We are all aware that young people have their own communication systems but the information they receive may be out of context and influenced by personal agendas.

Young people need to be involved in the admission process. Giving responsibility to the group for organising how they will welcome a young person to their home will have huge benefits for everyone. The young person feels wanted and valued and the existing group feel included and involved in the process. Simple reminders of how they felt when they first arrived *will* help sensitise them to the new young person.

Whilst we would not wish to be prescriptive there are times when a new arrival brings particular issues that have a particular impact, or potential for, on the group, for instance, stealing other people's belongings, setting fires in previous placements, associations with potentially dangerous people, drug/ alcohol use. Sensitively naming the behaviour with the young person and possibly within the group can help to create greater safety for all. We certainly have experience of the positive effects of such strategies and would encourage debate within teams on this.

Preparation of the young person

Within planned admissions the potential for creative and effective work with young people begins prior to their admission. Consistent with crisis intervention theory, at times of change the potential to make use of appropriate support for positive change is greatly increased. All change involves loss as well as possible gain. The loss that a young person will be feeling needs to be acknowledged in ways that assist their moving through the changes. Failure to do so will impede their progress. Resistance to change can become a significant feature. In this situation staff and young people can feel rejected and consciously or unconsciously react to this feeling of rejection in ways that can exacerbate the situation.

With current team sizes it can be overwhelming to meet the volume of new faces. This can be considerably eased by linking in two main staff who will be rotated on to significant shifts prior to and during the admission process. These staff will also assume responsibility for ensuring the practical arrangements for the new admission are met, for instance, preparation of the bedroom, buying the welcoming gift, ascertaining likes and dislikes in food and making sure the menu accommodates this, organising the file, co-ordinating and linking in key people like family, social worker, etc.

Communication tools

Staff in residential care are using a range of communication techniques with young people all of the time but very often these techniques are not formalised. At the pre-admission stage it is particularly important that staff are encouraged and enabled to consciously carry their tool bag with them. This may be to a setting they are unfamiliar with and carrying a deliberate plan with a range of ways to communicate this plan will help them approach the task in an appropriate, confident and empowering way. The use of techniques employed in life-story work for instance, will be particularly applicable. The use of family trees, lifelines, photostory work, cartoons, anti-colouring book, individual and family shields are a range of simple but effective ways in which communication can be facilitated. The potential for developing the tools of communication is enormous and once staff and young people engage in this work, development and refinement of the process will begin.

Care plans

Again these begin at the pre-admission stage. The pre-admission work needs to aim for agreements with young people about what kind of expectations the young person has of the home and vice versa. These will be highly individualised as well as general. So for instance a particular young person may have an issue about trust. He or she may voice a particular need to be trusted despite having being involved in activities which demonstrate trust to be an issue. The naming of the issue creates the opportunity to work out possible solutions to it. Helping the young person draw up their own agreement on what level of trust they feel they can handle at this particular stage will create achievable plans. One example of this at work was where a young person had stolen from his previous placement but never owned up to his action. By engaging him at the pre-admission stage, through the employment of a variety of communication techniques, he was able to name his own issues and work out ways to address these. He was clear that initially he could not trust himself. In another situation a young person was able to say that she wanted to be kept safe from a particular adult she was associated with. The naming of this allowed staff and the young person to work out what each could do in order to help keep her safe.

It is important to remind ourselves that an agreement, no matter how involved the young person is at the time, will very likely be broken. It is unrealistic to expect that by naming the problem and agreeing to a solution, that the problem goes away. Agreements therefore have to take account of what happens when they are broken or clearly not working. Work at particular stages, and especially prior to coming into a new placement, changes emphasis over time and therefore have to be flexible to change. It is particularly important that young people are allowed to make mistakes, as indeed staff are, but that the responsibility to address the mistakes is not avoided.

Care plans are part of a continuous process and therefore they need to be responsive to change. The Action and Assessment Records, published by the Department of Health, are becoming a central aspect of the care planning process. These take account of research findings which highlight significant areas of young people's lives that are all too frequently neglected in the lives of looked-after young people – health, education, identity and self-care. In actioning these records, staff need to be encouraged and enabled to use a range of communication tools that help the young person access the information detailed in the records. At first glance these forms can feel overwhelming. The skill in using them lies in the ability of staff to translate these into accessible formats. It is also important that the responsibility for meeting the needs of looked-after young people is not solely that of the residential staff. The organisation as a whole, working in partnership with the young person and their parents, needs to ensure that the records are used to their full potential. The Action and Assessment Records can help residential staff in supporting the message that this responsibility is owned by everyone.

Encouraging and promoting creative ways in which care plans are drawn up and communicated is vital to them being live, workable agreements which young people experience as useful and meaningful. This takes us to a discussion of the planning and review process.

Planning meetings and reviews

It is widely acknowledged that young people need to participate in the decisions being taken about their lives; however, formal arenas can be intimidating places in which to participate. Attention therefore needs to be focused on how these formal arenas can be made more accessible to young people and their families.

In interviewing young people about their experiences of these forums we have found them able to give some direction to staff on how they can be made more accessible. The following areas were highlighted by young people as needing more attention:

- Formal dress can be intimidating.
- A large number of people attending a meeting was experienced as intimidating.
- Refreshments were often seen as adult-centred.
- Meetings were experienced as being too long.
- The purpose of the meeting was not always clear to the young person.
- Young people felt their opinions took second place to those of adults.
- Some young people wished to have an advocate with them.

The comments made by young people in this particular survey were extremely helpful in shaping a forum which was more responsive to the needs of young people and more inclusive of their views. Gaining the views of young people can focus our attention on how to respond more effectively and creatively. For instance, a review report from a link worker and young person took the form of a collage. This provided a creative and accessible means of communicating to the review, which placed her views clearly at the centre of the review, thus reminding everyone of the purpose of the meeting.

It can also be advantageous for the staff and the young people to spend time away from the unit. A weekend away, for example, might facilitate improved communication and trust between staff and young people. The time away from the home provides a neutral space in which to work, a principle comparable to team away-days. The work in this context is facilitated by staff but led by the young people. Such work is demanding of time and resources, but in our experience it can help to facilitate the way in which staff and young people work together. There are benefits in enhancing group functioning and reducing conflict within the unit. Quite simply a group that functions well together creates the potential for developing safer, pro-active and positive environments for everyone. From here the potential to develop work with young people on their involvement and participation on all aspects of the residential unit is enhanced.

Young people's meetings

Many residential workers have recognised the need for young people to meet together on their own agendas and these forums have been in place within many residential environments for many years. This work has not, however, been recorded and written about. The 'Who Cares?' movement is perhaps the most accessible voice on young people's participation and involvement. The Children Act 1989 has recognised and formalised the need for young people's meetings and this has undoubtedly given weight to the work. But there is a need for staff to be guided and supported on how to provide a meaningful young person-centred meeting forum. In this section we hope to provide possible ways forward to achieve these.

Getting started

As with any form of group work, planning and preparing for the young people's meeting needs to take account of a number of factors before the group begins. Staff need to be clear who and what the group is for. When, where and how often it will meet? Who will be involved? In answering these questions it is important that staff are helped to put aside their own agendas, thereby approaching it from the young person's point of view. It is also important to be aware that young people will not necessarily have experience of this type of meeting and therefore they need to be enabled and encouraged to take up ownership of their own group. This is developmental, in that a new group will begin with a need for greater dependence on staff to take on a facilitative role. This role will have a clear aim towards creating a meeting forum which young people will eventually be able to facilitate for themselves. How this process unfolds will largely depend upon the stability of the group in terms of the speed and pace of the group's turnover. In short-term placements the role of staff will inevitably remain central. Generally, however, staff need to be working in ways which minimise their direct involvement over time.

Time out for the whole group – staff and young people – as described above can help to provide the foundation from which a young people's meeting can begin. This foundation needs to embrace the principles and philosophy of anti-oppressive practice in which difference can be celebrated. It is important that young people are helped to view their meeting from this starting point. By so doing issues of power and abuse can be addressed as a central part of the group's function. Staff need to retain the role of monitoring the group in relation to these issues; misuse of power cannot and should not be tolerated within young people's forums in the same way that it is not acceptable within staff teams.

Venue

Young people need to be able to choose their own meeting place. There may be a disused room or old staff house which could be adapted as a meeting place for young people. Such a room can become valued and developed by the young people.

Frequency

Young people need to be given support in deciding how often they wish to meet. When a new group is meeting it is important to create a momentum which can then be maintained over time. We would therefore suggest that young people are encouraged to try a series of meetings at weekly intervals – a position which can be reviewed once the young people have gained some experience.

Who should attend?

All young people who are resident in the unit should be encouraged to attend the young people's meeting. Inevitably some young people will be keen to attend and others will need encouragement. Attendance could be encouraged by attendance being mentioned as part of the placement agreement.

In terms of staff attendance there are a number of ways this can work. There are benefits both to having one constant staff member attending and to rotating staff attendance. In deciding which model is most suitable, staff need to take into account issues of consistency and follow through as well as holidays and rota arrangements.

Content

As we stressed earlier, within a young people's meeting it is important that it is the young people themselves who set the agenda. Initially, at least, young people need support in doing this. The use of role play, flipcharts and idea storming, games, videos and so on can be helpful in enabling young people to carry out this task. Staff involved in the process need to be clear about suspending their own adult agenda in order to make space for the young people. But it is also important not to set young people up to fail. They therefore need guidance about what is negotiable and what is not and where to take any demands they may have.

In the early stages of a new group it is important to experience a degree of success. It is therefore the role of staff to help steer young people on an achievable course. Addressing issues 'in house' that are achievable is a good starting point. So in one example the young people wanted to negotiate how they are woken up in a morning. As a result of discussions they all chose to have their own alarm clocks with individual responses negotiated if these failed to get them up. This was easily actioned and young people experienced a change, as indeed did staff, in a previously hazardous area, as a result of their inputs. In another example the group of young people requested a weekend away; they were helped to put forward a plan to the team meeting for this and the weekend went ahead. Once the group has experienced some successful outcomes from their meeting, not only can this increase the resolve to carry on meeting but also it can encourage their participation in more complex and less predictable areas.

Participation through the young people's meeting can be encouraged in a number of forums, for instance, the registration and inspection of their home, quality assurance forums, complaints procedures, selection and recruitment of staff. All of these are of central importance to the lives of young people in residential care but can so easily be divorced from them. The challenge, therefore, is to find ways of meaningfully involving young people in these crucial forums. As we have suggested, these need to be tackled in bite-sized chunks within a clear framework which values and communicates anti-oppressive practice.

Anti-bullying strategies

Bullying is endemic within society and not something which necessarily ends when school-leaving age is reached. Workplace harassment policies are increasingly recognising this fact, hence the introduction of wider-reaching definitions.

Bullying is also one of the main reasons young people run away from residential care (Rees 1994). It is therefore important that staff teams have clear strategies for dealing with bullying behaviour. As always, the starting point must begin with the staff team. How do staff relate to one another at times of disagreement and conflict? This question is particularly pertinent within the context of hierarchy within the team. If senior staff use bullying behaviour with team members this will be likely to become part of the culture for dealing with problematic behaviour. Young people take their cue from staff and we cannot stress this too strongly in this context.

It is a necessary starting point for staff teams to explore bullying within the team context. Bullying is an highly emotive issue and everyone will have experience of either being bullied and/or being a bully at some time in their lives. It is therefore important that attention is given to this personal experience – in doing so it will help staff to move on from a time in their life when bullying was an emotive issue, thereby enabling them to address the issues with and for young people within a professional context.

Managers and senior staff have a particular responsibility to create a culture where they can be challenged without fear of repercussion. In turn, staff will be more able to accept challenges from young people without reacting in abusive ways. This is particularly pertinent to the recent exposure of the abuses in residential care where male abusers used their power to intimidate young people whom they were abusing.

Bullying in residential care environments can easily go unchecked because it actually operates to keep control for staff. The familiar scenario is where the bully within the young people's group takes on the role of 'staff member' and inappropriately checks the behaviour of other young people. This role can be seductive for staff, especially in environments where so much energy can be diverted into keeping control of a difficult group. The young person may adopt the staff ethos of the home and as a result the young person can be seen as helpful and rewarded by the staff. This might not be conscious on the part of the staff but still operates to support and condone bullying behaviour. It is imperative that staff teams are enabled to stand back and check their environments with this kind of behaviour.

Anti-bullying strategies are distinct from the anti-oppressive practices already covered in this section. The reason that we stress this is because bullying is so endemic within society that young people will bring bullying or victim behaviour with them and this needs particular attention.

Once the staff team has had the opportunity to work through their own issues on bullying and appropriate responses to it, the next stage is to carry this forward into the young people's group. It may be helpful at this stage to check what work, if any, has been done in the schools that the young people attend: to build on existent awareness can only be helpful. As with the staff team, young people will bring their own life experiences of this emotive area and this will be an important starting point to move on from. There are a number of ways in which to access this information and many schools have materials that staff may be able to borrow. This approach also takes blame and guilt out of the subject, which is particularly important since we know that bullying behaviour lowers self-esteem for both victim and perpetrator.

Ultimately the aim should be for an anti-bullying policy which young people are involved in devising and therefore have ownership of. This is a lengthy and ongoing process where the naming of bullying behaviour is a positive start. Identifying bullies helps to keep it from going underground, where bullying often thrives.

An environment where bullying thrives can never be an empowering environment.

Sanctions in residential child care

The issue of sanctions in residential child care is a pertinent one for discussion, particularly in the light of disclosures about abuse within these environments. All organisations which administer residential child care must ensure that they have a policy on sanctions which is consistent with the guidance and regulations as set out in Volume Four of the *Guidance and Regulations on the Children Act 1989*. Whilst the exercise of these regulations is monitored through monthly managerial visits and annual registration and inspection, these checks alone are not sufficient to ensure that sanctions are being used appropriately.

Within residential environments where attention has been given to promoting positive practice which involves all young people, the need for sanctions will be reduced. Inevitably sanctions will still be necessary and it is necessary to ensure that these are negotiated with individual young people as well as with the group as an whole. Failure to involve young people in this process can result in sanctions being either useless or dangerous. It is through negotiation and participation that workable, meaningful responses become possible. This process also helps to break down barriers between staff and young people about the whole issue of control. The issue of control has particular tensions inherent within it which have intensified since the abuse scandals in residential child care began to emerge. Understandably this has resulted in some staff feeling very unclear about what is and what is not permissible control.

Staff need to be clear what the purpose of sanctions are and this needs to be evidenced by their effective use. The need to ensure as much safety, care and respect as possible for all young people is at the heart of any sanctions policy. Within this context it is helpful that a sanction has a place and a meaning to the individual young person receiving it and to the group as a whole. Disruptive behaviour towards the building may be an indication that the young person does not feel a part of the home. An appropriate sanction in this instance could be the decoration of a room or making something for the home.

Central to the issue of effective control is staff working alongside the young person in a supportive way. Not only does this involve the young person within the life of the home but it also signals to the other young people that their home is valued. It must also be remembered that a sanction that works in one particular instance may not work in another. For instance, taking money from pocket money for reparation for damage may be applicable for one but inappropriate for another. Within care planning, these kind of issues need to be examined pro-actively with young people. In one instance money was highlighted as a real issue for one young man. It was clear that to fine him would not have any impact, indeed it could lead him into more trouble. This was taken into account when the need for sanctions arose. Feedback from him on this revealed that he was facing up to the consequences of his actions in a way that he had not previously done. Having invested in the home initially through the use of a sanction which involved gardening, he began to take over this area of responsibility and showed pride in doing so.

Conclusion

In this chapter we have focused on the empowerment of young people on residential care settings. This began by setting the wider context within which residential care is located. We have given consideration to a number of key areas which we hope has opened up discussion and provided signposts for further work. We have not attempted to provide an exhaustive blueprint for residential work, but hopefully a starting point for residential staff to develop empowering practice. We now go on to examine in more detail the legislative and policy context provided by the Children Act 1989.

4 The Children Act 1989 and residential child care

Introduction

The Children Act 1989, implemented 14 October 1991, and the related guidance (Volume Four), provides the current legal and regulatory framework for residential child care in England and Wales. The Children Act is therefore central to the major concerns of this book. In this chapter we examine the content and impact of the Children Act, examining in particular the potential of the Act for contributing to the empowerment practice which we promote. In the second half of the chapter we examine in detail the issue of 'quality' which, largely stimulated by the Children Act, provides the contemporary context for service development within residential child care.

The background to the Children Act

The Children Act 1989, was devised in a period of great change for child welfare in England and Wales. Historically we have seen a major upheaval in child welfare legislation just about every 20 years – the years 1908, 1933, 1948, 1969 and 1989 all saw the passage of major child welfare legislation (Frost and Stein 1989).

It can be argued that the decade of the 1980s, in which the Children Bill was drafted and debated, was probably the most positive for residential child care for some time. As the raw statistics illustrate, the number of children and young people living in residential settings had declined steadily since the 1960s. As we saw in Chapter 1 this empirical decline was associated with what we might call an ideological decline. First, there was the impact of the permanence movement. Influenced by *Children Who Wait* (Rowe and Lambert 1973), social workers had become aware of the danger of 'drift' in care, that is children and young people in the care system without any clear, permanent plan for their future. Permanence usually implied either a rapid return home, or, failing that, a permanent care placement – through adoption or long-term fostering. This movement which was dominant for much of the 1970s and 1980s tended to put residential child care at the bottom of the priority list.

As we saw in Chapter 2, looking at theoretical perspectives, the influence of permanence was combined with that of the anti-institutional thinking of the 1960s. The seminal study in this field was Erving Goffman's study *Asylums* (1961). The studies of Goffman and related authors suggested that institutions could have a negative impact on human behaviour and that institutional practices could encourage long-term dependency. While the 1960s studies tended to be of mental institutions or prisons, there can be little doubt that these studies influenced the thinking of social workers and others towards children's homes. A further major factor was the economics and ideology of foster care which was privileged by the 1948 Children Act. Foster care was viewed as being able to help avoid the perceived impact of the institution and had the advantage of mimicking the family – almost universally regarded as the best environment for raising children and young people.

The impact of all these, and probably other factors, all coalesced to bring about a decline in the use of residential child care through the 1970s and 1980s. By the beginning of the 1980s it seemed that residential child care was in constant and unavoidable decline. In 1980 there were about 29,000 children in local authority-provided residential care; by 1992 this had declined dramatically to 7,600.

All this added up to a negative environment for the development of residential child care. In contrast, however, the lead up to the Children Act occurred in a more positive environment – therefore it is apparent that something began to change in the 1980s. What was this 'something'?

First, the voice of consumers began to be heard. The National Association of Young People in Care (NAYPIC) and other local groups of young people began to identify residential child care as a positive option for young people. This view was expressed in particular by older young people, those who had strong links with their families, by those who wished to live with siblings and those who had experienced serial fostering breakdown (see Rowe et al. 1989). Here we had a constituency for residential child care: young people wanting residential care as a positive choice and option.

Second, and unsurprisingly given our first point, researchers began to pick up some of the issues which young people had been raising . The Department of Health funded a wide range of child care research in the early 1980s which was brought together in the Department publication *Social Work Decisions in Child Care* (1985). The work of Packman (1986) and Fisher et al. (1986) in particular, began to challenge the established view that 'success' meant keeping someone out of care and 'failure' was defined by someone becoming looked after. The researchers suggested that this definition was resented by parents, who saw themselves as having to go 'through hoops' before gaining access to residential services for their children. It followed that residential care could be seen as a positive service, a service which people actually wanted and which could play a positive role. A model already existed for such a service: respite care for children and young people with disabilities. This service seems to be welcomed by parents as non-stigmatising and 'preventive' – indeed the fact that the service exists allows families to remain together often in difficult circumstances.

Third, and here we have a paradox, the emergence of 'scandals' which told us about problems in residential child care, led to a determination to improve it (see Chapter 8). The scandals concerning 'Pindown' (Levy and Kahan 1991), involving Frank Beck (Kirkwood 1993), and in North Wales (Williams and McCreadie 1992) were all known or emerging as the Children Act was conceived. There is a long history of major change in child welfare coming about as the result of 'scandals', most notably of course in the area of child protection (see Parton 1985). As we shall see later these scandals led, directly or indirectly, to a considerable momentum for reform.

Fourth, by the mid-1980s, it was becoming clearer to policy makers that whilst fostering clearly had a positive role to play, this role would be enhanced if fostering was specified and purposeful. Some young people were experiencing serial fostering breakdown which was damaging to all parties involved (Berridge and Cleaver 1987). It could therefore be argued that fostering services could not meet the needs of all young people and that fostering services need to be supplemented by the provision of a well-resourced, adequately staffed and targeted residential service (Berridge 1994).

Here then we have a number of forces which come together to challenge the 'dominant ideology' of the previous decades – that residential child care was inevitably a failure and a dumping ground. The service had internalised this image, defining itself as second best and sometimes as a dumping ground. The forces which have been identified above began to challenge this way of thinking and a more positive approach to residential child care emerged. The Children Act became an opportunity for making this emerging view reality. As the Utting Report (HMSO 1991a) stated:

> My main conclusion is that the new legal framework, and the regulations and guidance which go with it, provide a radically new framework which, if fully used,

should both oblige and help local authorities and others address ... problems effectively. (1991a: 23)

Here then we can see that the climate for residential child care began to turn around. At the beginning of the 1980s one would have estimated that residential child care was in almost terminal decline; by the end of the decade, while still facing serious problems, residential child care was probably the most actively discussed area of child welfare and subject to a whole series of state initiatives.

The Children Act 1989

We can now move on to look at the Children Act 1989, and assess the legislative impact of this new climate. First of all it needs to be said that the Act has to be seen as a whole – we cannot simply read those aspects of the Act that relate specifically to residential child care. The role of residential child care needs to be understood within the context of the Children Act in general.

A key idea in the Act is that of 'accommodation' and the related concept of children and young people being 'looked after'. These ideas represent a fundamental shift away from the previous ideas of compulsory and voluntary care. It was this framework which had fallen into disrepute and which needed to be rethought. The idea of accommodation reflected this – accommodation could be seen as a service, a positive resource which could have positive outcomes. As already stated, respite care provided a model for this more optimistic approach.

The idea of offering accommodation under Section 20 of the Children Act represented a major challenge to one of the most flawed aspects of the previous legislative framework – the misnamed idea of 'voluntary care'. As many parents could testify, this 'voluntary care' could all too easily become 'involuntary care', thereby bringing the whole idea into disrepute. As we have seen the Children Act needs to be seen as a whole – and the concept of 'parental responsibility' found in Section Five of the Act has a major role to play when we look at the provision of accommodation. The Children Act sees parents as continuing to play a key role once their children are accommodated – they continue to have parental responsibility and therefore, in theory at least, should play a major role whilst their children are accommodated. This makes the delivery of residential child care in partnership with parents and families possible.

The Children Act therefore restructures the population of residential child care. Basically, children and young people are now either subject to Care Orders under Section 31, having suffered 'significant harm', or are accommodated under Section 20. However, whichever legal category they come into they are all 'looked after'.

The key sentence in the Children Act in relation to residential child care does not immediately give us much information:

The Secretary of State may make regulations –

(a) as to the placing of children in community homes
(b) as to the conduct of such homes; and
(c) for securing the welfare of children in such homes.

In this seemingly technical Section is the legal basis of Volume Four of the Guidance and Regulations relating to Residential Care (Department of Health 1991b). It is to this crucial volume that we will now turn our attention.

Guidance and regulations

Volume Four of the Children Act Guidance and Regulations relates to residential child care and provides a comprehensive and detailed guide to the administration and management of residential child care. They form a basis for good practice and together with the SSI publication on standards in residential child care give us a baseline for good practice in residential child care.

In studying Volume Four we need first of all to make the distinction between 'guidance' and 'regulation'. This issue is best summed up by the Department of Health guidance:

Regulations say 'You must/shall'; codes say that 'You ought/should'. When the guidance explains regulations, it reaffirms the 'you must' messages. However, when it goes beyond regulations in setting out good practice, it conveys the message that 'It is highly desirable to...' or 'Unless there is a good reason not to, you should...' rather than 'You must'. (HMSO 1989: 2–3)

In reading and applying Volume Four this distinction must be held centrally in mind. The practice outlines provided in Volume Four, though now a little dated, nevertheless provide a sound basis for residential practice.

After Volume Four

An understanding of the current state of residential child care cannot end with the publication of the Children Act Guidance and Regulation. Immediately following the publication of the Volume residential care still found itself in a dynamic and changing climate including the following to name but a few of the numerous initiatives which relate to residential child care:

- The publication of the Utting Reports (1991 and later 1997)
- The publication of the Warner Report (1992)
- The draft and final permissible forms of control regulations
- The Residential Child Care Initiative for qualifying training
- The publication of the Department of Health review of research
- The publication of SSI standards for residential child care services (1994)
- The work of the Residential Taskforce.

These initiatives all served to assist the implementation of Volume Four and of the recommendations made by the first Utting Report. All this activity reflected the new agenda for residential child care: a higher profile, increased interest from government, local authority and voluntary bodies and considerable effort being put into improving the provision of residential child care.

The impact on residential child care

What has the impact of this mass of activity been? This complex question is addressed to a degree by this book (see also Sinclair and Gibbs 1998, and Berridge and Brodie 1998 for recent studies). What is certain is that some things have fundamentally changed since the decline and neglect of the 1960s and 1970s. These positive policy initiatives include the following: first, we have a new legal and regulatory framework; second, there is renewed emphasis on staff development and training; third, residential establishments are now subject to regular inspection, clear standards and Statement of Purpose have been established and, finally, staff recruitment has been reformed.

This new climate represents a challenge to managers and practitioners in residential child care. A new environment of change and challenge exists where it is the duty of all those with an investment in child welfare to grasp and develop these opportunities. We return to this challenge in our final chapter.

The quality agenda

One of the themes which unites many of these initiatives is that of *quality*. We shall now go on to examine the quality movement in the public sector in general and then move on to look at quality in residential care specifically.

Quality in the public sector

During the 1980s we saw the emergence of quality as a primary issue for the public sector in the UK. This concern emerged following the historic defeat of social democracy in the election of May 1979 (see Frost and Stein 1989). This defeat of the social consensus around the welfare state was very significant. It raised questions about the role of the state and the role of welfare which went to the roots of welfare provision in a modern state.

The Conservative government responded to the issues both through privatisation and through the establishment of regulatory regimes. Stronger forms of inspection and quality control were established through reformed inspectoral regimes, most notably in school-based education, and the Citizen's Charter initiative which sets specific standards in many areas of the public sector.

How can we define the concept of quality which lies at the heart of many of these initiatives? The British Standard defines quality as 'the totality of features and characteristics of a product or service which bear upon its ability to satisfy stated or implied needs'. Osborne states that in the human services 'a good quality service must be both fit for its purpose, and excellent in experience' (1992: 439). Whilst these definitions are a useful starting point we need to develop them so that we can ask questions about who is making these judgements and how? In social welfare we will also be concerned with the issue of how things are done: '*how* things are done is important both to users and outcomes – and therefore matters to Quality' (Wilding 1994: 59).

A young person in a children's home, for example, needs not only 'quality' food, but also to be involved in decisions about shopping and cooking. As Wilding also points out, quality is not an objective standard – what is quality for one user may not be quality for another user. This makes quality in the public sector very difficult to define and to implement.

When we think of quality in the public sector our gaze is soon directed to management – and the management jargon of 'Total Quality Management' or 'managing for quality'. There seems to be a consensus that the pursuit of quality and effective management are closely associated. Further management theorists argue that an organisational culture must make its primary goal the achievement of quality – and this must be achieved through teamwork. We can see therefore that a discussion of quality soon begins to make connections with the other issues we have discussed in this book. Quality cannot stand alone in splendid isolation.

Striving for quality also involves two distinct activities: quality control and quality assurance. Quality control allows us to recognise strengths and weaknesses in service delivery through evaluation and inspection. Quality assurance involves methods for assuring that the best quality services are delivered by actively minimising 'the likelihood of poor quality services being produced' (Osborne 1992: 441). For quality to be achieved we must also have specific standards set: 'standards of work and practice for staff and the goals to be achieved by the organisation. Everyone needs standards and goals as guides and targets' (Osborne 1992: 441).

These have now been clearly established in the residential child care sector by the Social Services Inspectorate (1994). In this sector, as well as others, one way of assessing whether or not these standards are being achieved is through inspection. Inspection in itself is of course necessary but not sufficient. Inspectors' reports may be left to gather dust and the findings must be integrated into the management system if they are to effect change.

The challenge for the public sector is at its sharpest in relation to involving users in the quality process. When we shop in Marks and Spencer's we are probably not too interested in being involved in their quality assurance mechanisms – in the market-place we can register our opinions through our expenditure. If there is a poor service we can shop elsewhere. This is normally not the case in the public sector, and in child welfare more particularly. Whilst young people often vote with their feet, we do not yet have a market-place where young people in care can exercise their consumer sovereignty. It is therefore crucial that service users are stakeholders in the quality process.

This is a problem where service standards have been set down by external bodies, such as the SSI. How can we truly say that we are involving users when the standard is already set? This suggests that such standards should be used as a starting point, to which users can contribute. Users should be involved then at a number of stages:

- Devising and developing standards
- Undertaking inspections
- Implementing changes to the service.

Thus the quality agenda can be an agenda which truly involves and empowers service users.

Quality in residential child care

We have outlined in the previous section the importance of the quality movement in the public sector. It can be argued that the quality issue is even more important in the specific service we are considering in this book. This is because children and young people in the care system are often severely disadvantaged prior to their entry to the care system; they are often reliant on the care system for their quality of life and are generally in a powerless position in relation to the adults who look after them. All these factors suggest that the involvement of young people in the quality process is of crucial importance.

What is the current state of the art? Let us take as our starting point the SSI publication *Standards for Residential Child Care Services*. The booklet was published in 1994 and is described as a 'catalogue of standards and criteria ... to support the SSI's programme of inspections of residential care services' (1994: iv). A standard is described as 'the quality of performance which is required in the management and delivery of social services if the service provision is to accord to the Department of Health policy and practice guidance' (1994: iv). Standards in turn are stated to 'derive from legislation, regulations and guidance, and current professional understanding (based on research and professional experience) of what constitutes good quality services' (1994: iv).

The publication suggests that there are nine appropriate headings, giving 36 standards in total. The nine headings include:

- Purpose and Function
- Children's Rights
- Child Protection
- Care of Children
- Quality of Opportunity
- Child Care Planning
- Premises
- Staffing
- Organisation and Management.

For each of the standards there are a number of criteria, 'more detailed and specific statements of expectation about particular aspects of a generally stated standard' (1994: v). The criteria themselves are divided into three sub-headings: 'Outcomes for Children', 'Home Practices' and 'Management Actions'. These three headings enable inspectors to make the links between Outcomes for Children (the experience and results of the service for children), Home Practices (how resources are mobilised to achieve aims), and Management Actions (how management facilitate effective child care).

Let us look in detail at just one standard to illustrate the point, 'Provision and preparation of meals'. The standard here states that 'Children are provided with adequate quantities of suitably prepared food having regard to their needs and wishes and have the opportunity to shop for and prepare their own meals' (1994: 42). Under the Home Practices section the SSI have established the following criteria:

- The home's routines for the purchasing of food, preparation and consumption of meals are flexible, and involve children

- That children help decide menus
- That children go shopping for food as part of the routine of the home
- That meals are orderly, well mannered, pleasant social occasions
- That individual preferences are catered for, and children are encouraged to try new dishes
- That food is provided in adequate quantities, is well prepared and presented and is wholesome and nutritious
- That there is reasonable choice at each meal, and that menus are varied
- That meals have regard to the cultural, racial and religious expectations of the children and represent ethnic culinary richness of the community
- That children may prepare their own snacks
- That there is suitable and sufficient catering equipment, crockery and cutlery available to provide for the needs of children accommodated in the home
- That there is proper facility for the refrigeration and storage of food
- That in large homes (more than 10 children) the design, layout, equipment, working practices of the kitchen satisfy standards laid down in food hygiene and food safety legislation and the Health and Safety at Work Act, 1974
- That in small homes (under 10 residents) kitchen facilities are available for use by the children, under appropriate supervision
- That in larger homes, where a non-domestic kitchen is required, there is domestic style equipment available for the children to use
- That staff responsible for food preparation confirm that they have achieved adequate and appropriate training
- That a significant number of meals take place in a socially rewarding manner appropriate to the group.

The detail of these prescriptions is striking – remember we have only outlined one section of one standard here. The SSI have therefore achieved a great deal in establishing a clear set of standards for residential child care workers to aspire to. In working with these standards we must however hold three factors in mind.

First, the difficulty in establishing standards is that these standards are in danger of being imposed on people. The challenge of establishing such standards is ensuring that children and young people remain active in interpreting the standards. An imposed standard remains an imposed standard no matter how high the quality demanded. The SSI are aware of this problem and have addressed this by ensuring that many of the standards focus on involving children and young people in the process – for example, of designing a menu. Another method of ensuring user involvement is by involving young people in the inspection process itself. This too contributes to ensuring that the standards do not become an end in themselves, but rather a means for ensuring that children and young people are actively involved.

Second, we need to be aware that standards will soon become out of date. The pace of change in modern society is so fast that standards which many of us adhered to, even a few years ago, now seem to be out of date and archaic. This is a major problem for the SSI who face the challenge of keeping standards across a wide range of services relevant and up to date.

Third, we cannot separate the quality issue in the public services from the wider debate about the funding and resourcing of the public sector. The achievement of the standards set out by the SSI are closely linked to a whole series of issues which are inseparable from funding issues. High-quality residential child care is dependent amongst other things on well-resourced buildings, motivated and well-trained staff, regular support and supervision, involved management, working within the Statement of Purpose and appropriate staff/young people ratios. As soon as we begin to examine these issues it becomes apparent that they are at least partly dependent on sufficient resources being available.

Conclusion

In this chapter we have examined the legal and regulatory basis of residential child care. This has led us to a discussion of the core issue of quality in residential child care. It is important to note however that law and regulation can only provide a framework for quality practice – it is sound managerial practice which strives to develop this framework to its full potential.

5 The management task in residential child care

The management role

The unit manager in residential child care has a complex, multi-faceted and fluid task. In this chapter we examine this task and suggest practical steps which the manager can take to ensure that the establishment functions effectively and efficiently to promote the welfare of children and young people who are resident. First of all, the manager must understand that their role is specific and differs from the role of other staff. One way of contributing to this distinction is to ensure that the manager is supernumerary to the rota – that is, that the normal rota is not dependent on the manager in order to maintain sufficient staff cover at any given time. This then provides the basis for the manager to undertake their crucial internal and external managerial duties. Internally the manager should be in a position to provide the necessary conditions which will promote the welfare of children and young people, including necessary support for staff. Additionally, however, there are also important external duties for the manager to perform. If the unit manager is not on the rota this enhances the possibility that the establishment itself will not become insular and inward looking. As we argue later in this chapter, this sense of connectedness with the outside world is one method of ensuring that best practice is promoted and that inappropriate, and sometimes abusive practices, do not grow up within the establishment.

We can imagine the manager's role as similar to that of a transmitter – sending important messages about residential child care policy and practice to the outside world and receiving important messages from the outside world, which are then disseminated to the staff team. In this way, the establishment remains in a dynamic relationship with the outside world, both contributing to and learning from developments in the wider world. This kind of activity provides stimulus and creativity for all involved parties. It provides knowledge and information which can help to create signposts for future development. The pro-active role of what we have called the transmitter can be empowering for all those with whom the manager relates.

Later in this text we examine strategies for ensuring that looked-after children and young people are empowered. For this to happen however it is important that staff themselves feel empowered and able to play this role with children and young people. In turn, for the manager to play a positive empowering role in relation to the staff team, the manager themselves must feel that they are empowered by the organisation. This raises a whole series of questions:

- Where does residential child care fit in with the overall Children's Services Plan?
- What role have managers had in developing the Plan?
- Do unit managers get a chance to meet together?
- Are their views listened to?
- Does the unit manager receive regular supervision and training?

A recent survey of newly qualified residential managers leaving an approved Residential Child Care Initiative route indicated that managers are clear about how they perceive their needs (Karban and Mills 1995). Once these needs are established it is up to their senior managers to ensure that such needs are clearly addressed. Organisations that are clear and pro-active about the role of residential child care can attract the high-quality staff needed to perform the residential task.

Let us now examine in more detail our conceptualisation of the unit manager as having inward-looking and outward-looking factors.

Outward-looking aspects

Outward-looking tasks will involve a whole range of contacts with the outside world, including contact with aspects of the local community, line managers with responsibility for the establishment, other parts of the organisation which the establishment is part of and agencies with which the establishment comes into contact. The Unit Manager forms the crucial link with all these aspects of the outside world: it is imperative that these outside relationships are approached in a planned and systematic manner. Let us examine each one in turn.

Links with the community

Most modern residential child care establishments will be situated in the heart
of their local communities. This has many advantages: looked-after young
people should be able to participate in the life of the local community in the
same way as other local people do. There will be barriers to this however. We
know that young people who are resident in establishments will face stigma
and prejudice and therefore staff will need to work creatively to help create
conditions in which young people can so participate.

Relationships with close neighbours can be highly problematic for residential establishments. Neighbours may complain about the real, or perceived,
behaviour of young people resident at the establishment. Sometimes the
establishment may get blamed for problems within the community which
might actually be nothing to do with the establishment. The establishment
must be pro-active and positive in building relations with local people. It is
our experience that many people have, at least initially, a residue of good will
towards young people in care. This good will needs to be mobilised and built
on by the establishment. It is helpful if contact is made with local people
apart from those contacts made in emergency or complaint situations. Visits
can be made to people's homes or, when it is felt appropriate by the young
people, local people can be invited into the establishment. Staff need to ensure
that positive relationships are established with people in the local community,
such as the local shopkeeper, newsagent and so on. These contacts can be
used to explain the role of the establishment, how the establishment works
and to outline how local people can communicate with the establishment
when the need arises. Thus local people can gain a positive view of the
establishment instead of perceiving it as having a negative impact on their
lives. Of course there will almost inevitably be situations where young people
are problematic for the local community – perhaps causing noise, disruption,
or being involved in crime. Where this happens it is important that the
establishment responds consistently and rapidly to any complaints from the
local community. Where incidents have occurred in the locality it is important
that young people are confronted with any responsibility they may have for
the events and where appropriate are asked to make reparation. We return to
issues of control in our section on empowering children and young people.

Links with other organisations

As well as what we might call the intra-organisational network the establishment will also find itself to be part of a broader network with outside
organisations. Such organisations might include the police, youth service,
libraries, schools, the health service, psychologists, psychiatrists and voluntary

organisations, to name but a few. Much of what we have already said about networks in general will apply here: this network is important and it needs to be worked at and nurtured.

The danger with external networks is that the establishment will only turn to them in moments of crisis. Psychologists and psychiatrists might be turned to when a young person is troubled, or the school contacted only when a young person is truanting. What is needed here is a more strategic approach which develops networks and builds relationships with other agencies on a creative basis and not necessarily in crisis situations. Again the unit manager will be central to this: it will be to the manager that primary responsibility falls to make and develop links with various agencies. The advantage of doing this strategically is that outside agencies can be facilitated in gaining a positive view of the establishment, appreciating its strengths and things that it does well. If agencies are only contacted in crisis it is inevitable that they come to view the establishment as problematic. These links can be built in a variety of ways: through open days; regular liaison meetings; and attending events organised by other agencies. The unit manager needs to make time to do this: the danger is always that today's 'crisis' will always take priority over the need to plan strategically and ensure that there is an investment in the long term, as well as the short term.

The establishment needs to take a pro-active approach to these aspects of liaison. The unit manager needs to take responsibility for these actions – it is no use waiting for others to make contact with the establishment. Again it is likely that this will only happen in negative, crisis situations. This is not to say that the unit manager should be the only person to play a liaison role: such roles can be appropriately delegated to other members of staff, but the responsibility for such delegation and for co-ordinating links must lay with the unit manager.

Additionally establishments can make useful connections with educational and research institutions. This can involve practice thinking, making inputs to diploma and other social work programmes, and involvement in research projects. These links will help to ensure that the manager is linked in with new thinking and cutting-edge developments in social work and social care. It is also a way of making sure that residential and group care issues are addressed on Dip.S.W. and related courses.

Links with the internal management of the organisation

The unit manager in a large statutory or voluntary organisation is likely to have three or more levels of management above them, each of which has potentially major influence over the establishment. The most direct contact is likely to be with a manager who has responsibility for a range of residential establishments, who we shall refer to as the Residential Management Officer. This is probably the most important relationship for the unit manager to negotiate as this level of management will act as the main conduit between the establishment and the rest of the organisation. The relationship between the unit manager and the residential management officer is quite often difficult. There is potential for conflict over the difficult issue of unplanned admissions. The residential management officer will often have responsibility for allocating such unplanned admissions and this can lead to conflict with the unit manager, who will be anxious to defend both their Statement of Purpose and the stability of their establishment at any given moment.

There is no easy answer to addressing this conflict: it can be seen as a structural conflict, that is built into the roles of the different managerial roles. The unit manager has a legitimate role in trying to defend their establishment from unplanned and potentially disruptive placements, just as the manager with responsibility for allocations must somehow find a suitable placement for the child or young person. These issues can be openly aired and discussed in residential management meetings where all the unit managers gather together with the residential management officer. This allows the issues to be discussed on a shared basis thus reducing the chances of the conflict becoming personalised and polarised. Such issues can be explored in more depth in away days facilitated by an independent outside person – a person who should have knowledge and experience of the residential field. By recognising and working within the structural constraints of their relationship it should be possible for managers with different levels of responsibility to maintain a positive and creative relationship.

The residential management officer will have responsibilities for the support and management of the unit manager, which are similar to those that the unit manager has for their staff. Additionally it needs to be recognised that the unit manager is in a potentially isolated position. When they are in the establishment the manager occupies a difficult role in being at once *part* of the residential team and *apart* from the residential team. This places the unit manager in the difficult position of having to make many decisions on the spot whilst being aware of their difficult and sometimes contradictory position. The unit manager will require particularly skilled supervision from their senior manager, and perhaps support from an external consultant, to ensure that they are handling this difficult position in a clear and coherent manner which their staff will be able to simultaneously comprehend and respect.

Above the senior manager with which the unit manager has immediate contact will be various levels of senior manager up to and including the Director or Chief Executive of the organisation. These managers will from time to time take crucial decisions which will impact on the establishment, particularly decisions relating to overall policy and resourcing. It is important therefore that the unit manager has a creative method of communicating with the senior management team. The unit manager will have basically two types of issues on which they wish to communicate with senior managers. First, there are shared issues which will demand collective communication from all unit managers within the organisation, for example, an issue relating to staffing levels in residential establishments. Second, there will be issues specific to their particular establishment, perhaps relating to incidents in the establishment or establishment refurbishment, for example.

First of all let us examine issues of collective concern to unit managers. In order to ensure that issues can be raised which are common to all establishments the basic requirement is that unit managers meet together on a regular basis. This will allow the managers to explore which issues they have in common and discuss the action which needs to be taken about them. In complex organisations, such as social service departments or large voluntary organisations, it is difficult for senior managers to give detailed attention to all aspects of the organisation's work: inevitably it falls to special interest groups, such as residential managers, to ensure that issues which concern them are raised appropriately through the managerial machinery. Sometimes it will be possible to raise issues simply through the accepted protocol of the line management system or by memo; on other occasions it may be necessary to campaign for the changes that the group wish to see. Whatever the situation it remains the case that a regular, well-attended and purposeful meeting of unit managers will be necessary.

Second, there may be issues which are more specific to the individual establishment. Again it may be possible to raise these issues by memo or through the line management system. Where this is possible it should be the first method used by the unit manager. On other occasions the unit manager might want to mobilise support for the particular change they are looking for. Depending on the situation this might involve mobilising support from the young people and their organisations, their team and perhaps the unions or professional organisations. Exceptionally the unit manager might want to lobby elected members or committee members.

It is apparent that whether the issue is shared or specific the unit manager requires contact with senior managers and therefore needs to be skilled in presenting their case either verbally or in writing, and in working with others to bring about change. In management terms while many of the tasks in the establishment will demand the unit manager is skilled in *operational* management, many of the issues we have discussed in this section will demand that the manager has *strategic* management skills. The unit manager will have to develop a long-term view of the role of their establishment and the issues which need to be in place for the establishment to work effectively in the future. Rising above the day-to-day problems and issues, the unit manager will have a view on long-term developments and how the establishment needs to be positioned in relation to these.

Links with other parts of the organisation

As well as the links with senior management which we have emphasised in the previous section, the establishment will also find itself at the centre of a complex network of relationships with other parts of the organisation. If the organisation is a social services department, for example, this network will include fieldworkers, inspectors, finance and administrative staff and specialist staff, such as reviewing officers or child protection staff. This network is important to the establishment for a number of reasons. First, the status and image of the establishment may well be generated by this network who will have direct knowledge of the establishment and how it operates. Second, positive relations with this network will offer great support to the establishment: they can potentially offer access to resources and expertise which can be the lifeblood of the establishment. Conversely if an establishment has negative relations within the network this can make the work of the establishment difficult. Third, this network offers one important link between the establishment and the outside world. This is important in breaking down the potential isolation of residential establishments and the danger of them becoming closed institutions.

Networks need to be worked at and maintained. The unit manager will have to lead on this, although it is also important to involve other members of staff where possible. A network may be enhanced and worked with in a number of ways which might include, for example, involving outside people in working groups to do with issues concerning the establishment or through social events. Investment in the network may well pay dividends later when, for example, the establishment needs to mobilise some special expertise or needs friends within the organisation.

We can see from this discussion that the establishment is at the centre of a complex web of individual and organisational contexts. Our main message is that the unit manager should take a pro-active stance towards this network. If a passive stance is taken then contacts with members of the network will tend to happen in negative or crisis situations. In addition, opportunities will be lost to build positive supports for the establishment.

Strategic work

The unit manager is responsible and accountable for the effective management of the establishment. A strategic view can only be taken where there is a clear conception of the purpose of the establishment. The Utting Report has highlighted the importance of the Statement of Purpose and this is now enshrined in the Children's Homes Regulations. The regulations stipulate that the Statement should outline 'The purpose for which the children's home is established, and the objectives to be attained with regard to the children accommodated in the home' (Children's Homes Regulations, 1991, Schedule 1).

It is this Statement of Purpose which gives the unit manager a focus for their strategic, as well as operational, skills. Strategically the Statement demands that the unit manager is able to locate the establishment in the correct strategic position in relation to wider policy within the organisation. The unit manager will have to keep an eye on shifts and changes in the organisation which may demand changes to the Statement of Purpose. Only if the establishment is efficiently managed in terms of this strategic position will it be possible for the establishment to be managed effectively on an operational level.

The Statement of Purpose also gives the establishment an opportunity to mobilise the network we have already referred to. Professionals, inside and outside the organisation, children and young people and their carers can be involved in helping to create, or where appropriate change, the Statement of Purpose. This will have the advantages of creating a sense of ownership amongst those involved as well as mobilising the knowledge and skills of network members in contributing to the Statement of Purpose.

It may also be possible for the establishment to contribute to strategic planning at an organisational or corporate level. This is the great opportunity offered by the Children's Services Plan. It should be remembered that this idea was given prominence by the first Utting Report (HMSO 1991a) which highlighted the need for integrated child care planning in local authority settings. Residential child care establishments need to ensure that their service is fully integrated into service planning at the organisational level.

This again illustrates the complexity of the residential management task. The unit manager is asked to operate at an operational level on a day-to-day basis in their establishment, strategically in relation to the establishment where the Statement of Purpose is contained and strategically on a broader basis in relation to the Children's Services Plan.

Inward-looking aspects

As well as these important outward-looking aspects of management, the unit manager must not lose sight of the issues of management which are concerned more directly with the operation of the establishment. It is important for the day-to-day management of the establishment that the strategic work we have outlined takes place. A sound Children's Services Plan (or overall policy statement in a voluntary or private organisation) and a clear and relevant

Statement of Purpose are essential if the establishment is to deliver a quality service. These form the foundations for residential child care establishments, and, as we argue in our final chapter the basis for high-quality child care more generally.

The crucial interface between the planning function of management and the operational function is the Statement of Purpose. The Statement of Purpose should provide the means by which the establishment can translate strategic requirements into operational goals. The reality is that the unit manager will often find themselves defending the Statement of Purpose. The Statement should specify the role of the establishment – this might be framed, for example, in terms of the age, gender or type of young person to be accommodated. Inevitably these specifications may be challenged by the organisation which may want to place a child or young person whose characteristics are not consistent with the Statement of Purpose.

If the unit manager is able to operate to the Statement this is a sound basis for the successful operational management of the establishment. It is not possible in a textbook such as this to outline the 'correct' way to respond to each and every situation which may face a unit manager, in what we have already identified as a complex and multi-faceted task. We can however attempt to set out the building blocks which need to be in place for a successful establishment (the supervision system, the Statement of Purpose, for example) and the principles which the unit manager can refer to in terms of the efficient management of the establishment. It is to these principles of operational management in residential child care that we now turn our attention.

Empowering the young person

In Chapter 3 we examined what we see as the central function of residential child care – that is to empower children and young people. This goal, if accepted, provides a useful guideline for managerial decision making – it provides a template against which the validity of a given managerial decision can be measured. Any given decision can be assessed against the question did this decision help to empower the children and young people who are resident in the establishment? For managerial decision making this has a number of advantages. First, as we outline below, we believe that empowerment is a helpful framework in guiding child care practice. Second, empowerment can be used to describe everyday, and seemingly minor decisions. For example, a decision to put staff meeting minutes on the notice board, whilst hardly revolutionary, can be seen as helping to empower. Third, managerial decisions can be empowering which might not be seen as immediately in agreement with the young person's wishes. For example, a decision to ask a particular young person to play their stereo more quietly will no doubt incur their displeasure, but can be seen as beneficial for the group and for developing the individual's sensibility to other peoples' needs. In this sense we see an empowerment framework as more useful than, say, a straightforward children's rights perspective. Fourth, and finally, an empowerment framework is helpful in assessing negative decisions. For example, let us say that organisational policy dictates that an establishment should drive a minibus with the organisation's name and logo on the side. Staff might resist this but in the end have to go along with it if their objections are ignored. This is clearly not empowering for the young people, but the staff group can be clear that this is a problem and something that they might be able to change in the long run.

In these ways then we would attempt to make connections between *management* decisions and *empowerment* of children and young people. This principle provides a sound basis for management decisions.

The handover

In residential child care the handover from one shift to the next, or from one staff member to another, is a crucial moment, and yet one which can be so easily overlooked. This moment is often highly charged. But if the emotional content of this moment is not given space and attention it can cloud thinking and subsequent action. For the staff coming on duty it is a moment filled with questions. These questions will have even more emotional significance if staff have been away for some time or if their last shift was particularly difficult. Questions such as: What has happened while I have been away? Have there been any disturbances? Is anyone missing? For the member of staff handing over the issue of tiredness may predominate and/or they may have had a particularly difficult shift and be filled with all kinds of feelings which will impact on how they hand over.

With this in mind it is important that the process is responsive to the emotional content. Strategies for handling this in positive ways in order that it does not negatively influence the new shift need to be developed. It can therefore be helpful to discuss this issue during staff meetings, where everyone has the opportunity to participate. In devising a handover process it is crucial that there is a place for the emotional content to be listened to and responded to. It may be helpful therefore for the staff coming on duty to take the lead in asking questions. For instance, what happened with x? How did you feel when it happened? How are you feeling now?

Another important point to note about the handover is how the young people respond to the staff being unavailable to them for this period. They may also have feelings about being talked about especially if they have been disruptive and this is handed over to the next shift. All residential staff will be familiar with the constant interruptions from young people, especially during weekends and school holidays. One possible way of minimising the tension for young people at this event is for them to be directly involved. This allows the young people to give their perspective on the last period from their point of view and to be part of any response to this. Another possibility is for one member of staff to remain with the young people during the handover period and discuss any issues with them.

Whatever shape the handover forum takes, it is important not to lose sight of its purpose which is to facilitate the consistent care of the young people and promote their welfare.

Selection and recruitment

Whilst the responsibility for the selection and recruitment of staff does not fall solely on the unit manager, their involvement is central to the process. The organisation as a whole needs to have a detailed, clear policy for this process. Guidance for developing such a process is provided by the Warner Report (HMSO 1992), and elaborated on in the second Utting Report (HMSO 1997). The need for a rigorous selection process is self-evidently crucial and one that lends itself to creative and pro-active developments where young people and staff can meaningfully participate. Selection of the best possible staff is central to providing a quality service where positive teams are built to work in residential child care.

The selection process has a number of important stages to it:

1.   Job descriptions and specifications form the first stage. These need to be clearly thought out and endorsed by the organisation as a whole.

2.   Posts must also be carefully and openly advertised. What messages does the organisation want to convey? Who is the advert trying to reach? Where is the best place to locate the adverts?

3.   The organisational process needs to support and facilitate the process of recruiting staff. What is the procedure for clearing vacancies? Are delays in the system detrimental to effective staff recruitment? Does the organisation recognise the disruption caused by the departure and arrival of staff in a group living context? It is the role of managers to communicate these messages to the organisation more widely and ensure that broader organisational practice is as supportive as possible to the needs of the residential child care service. The reality is that most senior managers will not have direct, or recent experience, of residential work and may not be aware of the pressures and realities. Unit managers therefore need to communicate effectively the importance of filling vacancies as quickly as possible.

4.   The interview process for residential staff needs to involve staff and young people. Preparation is the key and we would suggest that the training section of the organisation could provide support and preparation of the young people in this process. We have experience of a young people's panel being established which interviewed candidates and scored their performance as one element of the entire process.

5.   The diversity of the team in the residential child care setting should be regarded as an asset and should be actively promoted as part of the selection process. The aim should be to build a team with the necessary skills and experience to deliver the residential child care task. The emphasis on diversity allows teams to reflect the diverse nature of the community from which the young people will have come from and enable the team to develop a shared value base of child-centred, empowering practice. In short, diversity is an asset to be celebrated as a central aspect of the team.

Building and empowering the staff team

An effective manager will also want to build their team as this is the basis both for consistently empowering young people and for delivering a quality service. Only a motivated staff team will be able to provide high-quality care on a consistent basis for children and young people.

Staff teams are not built passively or by default. Team building is an activity which involves a pro-active stance and a strategic plan by the manager. It is also something that happens constantly – not an isolated activity which happens once a year on away days! There are many texts on team building (Wiener 1992, Payne 1982, for example) which we can only summarise here.

First, a team can only be motivated if they adhere to a clear and agreed task. This is why we have placed a high emphasis on the Statement of Purpose earlier in this chapter. A clear purpose allows the team to build their skills and expertise in relation to this task, and also enables them to measure their achievements and success.

Second, a team is best motivated if it is involved in decisions and policy making. The manager who adopts an open and inclusive decision-making process is more likely to find that the team are motivated and supportive.

Third, a team is a live and changing organism – this means that team building is never 'done', never 'finished'. The team manager is responsible for being responsive to these changes and aware of them. These changes need to be responded to and discussed.

Fourth, a quality team should not be equated with lack of conflict. All teams contain conflict within them: the test of a high-quality team is how conflict is handled by the team. Conflict can be negative and debilitating, or it can be stimulating and creative. Mechanisms need to be in place for ensuring that conflictual issues are aired, that staff are listened to, and that creative responses are put in place.

Fifth, a strong team also has a place for developing the individual – the team should not limit and restrain the skills and values of the individual. We focus on this issue in our discussion of support and supervision of staff.

Empowering management style

In this book we argue that empowerment is potentially the key concept in helping us understand and move forward residential child care. Many feminist management theorists have argued that empowerment management style is consistent with a feminist approach to management. Grimwood and Popplestone argue that empowerment is central to a feminine approach to management: 'they can develop "empowering" skills and limit their "controlling power"… Management as empowering can also mean sharing power with others' (1993: 139). By exploring such management techniques, however, in traditionally male-dominated organisations, women take many risks: 'to manage in a different way – like a woman – is to run the risk of being spotted as different, and of being ignored, ridiculed or overworked' (1993: 121–22).

There are tendencies within the management world, however, which are shifting what we might identify as the dominant management culture towards what we might call a feminist or empowerment model. Mainstream management theorists such as Peters and Waterman (1983) argue that managers must enable and support, rather than placing the emphasis on control and regulation. It may be then that what Grimwood and Popplestone describe as 'women's preference for teamwork and collaborative working' (1993: 118) is being shifted into the mainstream and that this is reflected in management theory and hopefully increasingly in practice.

Conclusion

We can see from this chapter that the managerial task in residential care is complex and multi-faceted. We have attempted to focus on this by examining the outward-looking and inward-looking role of the manager. We have attempted to locate managerial skills in relation to our key organising concept of empowerment – both the empowerment of the staff team and of children and young people. Our basic approach is consistent with the findings of Sinclair and Gibbs (forthcoming) in their recent extensive study. They conclude:

Evidence suggests that social services who wish to produce high staff morale in their children's homes should:

- Enhance the status, job security and career prospects of their staff
- Develop staff roles, including possible after-care and work with families
- Empower the heads
- Develop training which enhances rather than disrupts a common approach
- Encourage regular formal supervision.

It is this latter point that we explore in our next chapter.

6   Supporting and supervising staff

Introduction

As we have seen in the previous chapter the need for high-quality support, supervision and management is widely acknowledged within social care practice, policy and training (see Sinclair and Gibbs 1998, for example). Within this wider context however, residential and group care settings have frequently suffered due to this general acknowledgment not being actively applied and pursued. It is not uncommon for residential staff to be unclear about the role and purpose of formal supervision or indeed have little or no experience of receiving it – high quality or otherwise. As the Warner Report observed: 'Many employing authorities report that the bulk of supervision is "informal". By this we can only assume that it is unplanned, ad hoc and irregular' (HMSO 1992).

In recent years this deficiency has begun to be acknowledged and has been addressed in much of the official literature (Howe 1992; HMSO 1991; Skinner 1991; Warner 1992). As we have argued in Chapter 4 this 'post-Children Act' climate provides the basis for the improving standards and practice within residential child care.

In this chapter we shall address the role of the unit manager specifically in relation to aspects of staff support and supervision. It is our contention that supervision is a central element in building an empowering environment and can be part of a package of support to staff which helps to provide a positive working environment. Sinclair and Gibbs (forthcoming) argue that staff satisfaction is 'enhanced if they felt they had a clear role, good support from their colleagues and management, adequate money, security and job prospects, and their work did not interfere too much with their family and social lives'.

Supervision

We would argue that supervision is crucial to establishing, developing and maintaining high-quality residential child care environments. Recent literature has placed a strong emphasis on the importance of supervision (Hawkins and Shohet 1989; Payne and Scott 1982; Frost and Harris 1996). We would argue that effective supervision, when delivered within a clear framework, is empowering to staff and therefore to young people also. As we have suggested elsewhere in this book the route to the empowerment of young people is via the effective empowerment of the staff team.

First let us explore further what supervision involves, before we move on to consider how it might best be applied in residential and group care settings. The British Association of Counselling provide a definition which gives us a clear focus for understanding the centrality of supervision and a standard against which the quality of supervision can be measured: 'The primary purpose of supervision is to protect the best interests of the client' (British Association of Counselling 1987: 2). Within this broad definition it has been argued that high-quality supervision should have three identifiable aspects. These have been identified by Kadushi (1976) as educative, supportive and managerial. Let us consider each of these aspects in more detail.

Educative

Supervision provides an educative vehicle through which practice can be informed and developed. It is through effective supervision that relevant theoretical concepts can be introduced, discussed, debated and developed into a practice model. For example, let us take a link worker who has the task of planning a series of meetings between a young person and her family. Supervision provides an opportunity to explore the relevant theoretical concepts which can then shape and inform this particular piece of practice. Issues such as the law and research relating to family contact can be examined as well as the practicalities of ensuring that the meetings go well and that the young person is supported in dealing with any issues which arise. With the knowledge base in place, supervision can then be used to plan how to approach the task, including the identification of the necessary skills, resources and support required in order to successfully complete the task of arranging the meeting between the young person and her family. Finally supervision would also be the forum for monitoring the progress of work and to identify key learning points and any further training and development needs.

Supportive

All of us learn best within a supportive environment. We would also argue that a supportive framework is central to the empowerment model which is the key connecting theme of this book. It follows that if staff experience supervision as a supportive event they will be encouraged to carry this model forward into their direct work with young people. Thus a positive and supportive environment for supervision can have a direct impact in helping to create a supportive environment for young people. Being supportive does not only mean approving all that is done by the worker, but also being honest and open about any shortcomings in a worker's performance. This will also have the effect of highlighting training and staff development needs. To be most effective such a supervisory relationship needs to exist within the context of properly resourced and managed staff development and appraisal systems.

Managerial

It is the managerial aspect of the supervision process which makes it distinct from other forms of supervision considered later in this chapter – such as peer support or consultation. The supervisor is charged with the responsibility to ensure that the supervisee meets required standards of practice. This form of supervision therefore includes within it an element of accountability. Managerial accountability can present difficulties within the supervisory relationship – it can dominate the process or, in contrast, be fudged and inadequately addressed. It is an issue, however, which needs to be balanced within the context of a supportive and educational supervisory relationship.

In order to perform the managerial role within supervision there needs to be clarity about the residential task and the individual and team roles and responsibilities in carrying out this task. As we have already stated, a staff development or appraisal system can effectively set out a framework for establishing strengths and weaknesses, and to identify the training and developmental needs of individual staff members. Within this there needs to be a clear understanding of what the acceptable standards are and what action needs to taken if standards are not being met. Supervisors therefore need to be aware of what the organisational response would be and the process to follow if standards are not met. To give an example, if it was agreed that a worker was not competent within the residential setting what redeployment opportunities are available?

The challenge for managers therefore is to ensure that supervision is consistently provided, of high quality and is well planned. To support this process the organisation has responsibilities to ensure that necessary resources and support are available.

The supervision process

Having considered these three dimensions of supervision, it is important to understand that the supervision process can only be understood as a two-way process in which both the supervisor and the supervisee each have a responsibility to engage in a meaningful manner. It is also a process to which both will bring a certain amount of 'baggage' – by this we mean their previous experiences and views of supervision. This will contain any previous negative experiences of supervision – perhaps previous supervision has been chaotic, unplanned and unreliable – and may also include misconceptions about its purpose. But whatever these issues are they need to be directly addressed and discussed within the supervisory relation.

In group care settings there are exciting opportunities for the supervision process to take place in a number of different formats, not only individual but paired or team-based, for example. Developing these possibilities allows supervision to reflect and be sympathetic to the dynamic nature of the group care setting. Before examining these different formats let us examine the supervisory relationship.

The supervisory relationship

Central to the residential child care task is the use of interactive and interpersonal skills and the ability to work through even the most difficult relationships. Communication is therefore a key tool: 'Good communication and support need to be seen not only as a science, but also as an art form' (Baldwin 1989: 164).

While clarity about the role and function of supervision comes from a well-planned supervision programme, the relationship between the supervisor and the supervisee will be crucial to the successful delivery of a positive supervision programme. The relationship needs to be built on the basis of trust, honesty, reliability and respect. The responsibility for initiating this process of relationship building rests with the supervisor. Not only will this have positive effects in supervision but it also serves as a role model for staff which they will be able to reflect in their work role.

The supervisor is in a powerful position in relation to the supervisee. The supervisory role carries organisational power, sanctioned in order to ensure that the service is adequately delivered. Whilst the supervisee may have a certain amount of personal power, the power dynamic is nevertheless weighed towards the supervisor. There is a parallel here with the power invested in staff in relation to young people. This power can be used positively or negatively. If used positively the worker will be empowered, encouraged and enabled to work effectively together with the young people. If used negatively the outcome is the opposite; the worker will lose self-esteem, and this will be picked up by the young people, who will in turn lose self-esteem and confidence. This might show itself, for example, by concentrating on the negative behaviour of the young people, as a mirror image of the way that supervision operates. Or, if boundaries between the supervisor and the supervisee are unclear or too rigid, this again can be mirrored in relationships with the young people.

It is important that the supervisor acknowledges the power balance in the supervisory relationship and uses it wisely, safely and appropriately. The benefits will be evident both within the relationship and more widely in the unit.

It is essential that supervision is experienced as an empowering event, and is then translated positively into the staff's relationship with the young people. This role-modelling is both central and crucial to the residential child care task – where the contact between practitioners and young people is both extensive and intensive.

While we have outlined what we see as the basis for a high-quality supervision programme, it must be recognised that for this to work it is at least partly dependent on the availability of the necessary resources. First, teams need to be sufficiently staffed to meet the minimum standards established by the Social Services Inspectorate (1994).

Second, the team need to work to a clearly defined Statement of Purpose, so that they can build their skills around a clear task to which everyone is committed. Third, the team need to work in a positive physical environment which provides the material base for their direct practice. Fourth, the necessary skills have to exist in the team. This needs to developed through good employment practice, high-quality training and effective recruitment and retention of staff. These factors will provide the overall context in which quality supervision can be developed.

Holding these factors in mind we shall now go on to develop the basis of a supervision process in a residential unit:

1. The foundation and starting point for a supervision policy is for the team to work towards building a shared philosophy for the care of children and young people within the unit. This should be explicit and outlined in the unit Statement of Purpose.

2.　It needs to be clear within the team exactly what the residential task is in the specific setting.

3.　The supervision plan should be linked to a coherent appraisal programme.

4.　The team should agree how they see the role of supervision and the balance between the three aspects of supervision which we have already examined, that is, educative, supportive and managerial. This process will best be facilitated if sufficient time is given to it, and if it involves practical exercises (see Frost and Harris 1996, for examples of these).

5.　It is important to share experiences of supervision within the team. The aim of this should be to identify positive and negative aspects of supervision that people have experienced. Within the team context this exercise will give team members permission to share their doubts, fears and uncertainties about supervision. Within the collective, and hopefully supportive, context of the team it should be easier for team members to share any doubts than it would be in the one-to-one supervisory setting, where the power tends to be balanced towards the supervisor. This process can be followed up by creating a structure which allows the team to feedback on their supervision experience to an outside consultant or a member of the management team who is not their supervisor. Feedback can then be given to the supervisor which provides a dynamic element to the supervision process.

6.　It is also important that those with supervisory responsibility should formulate a personal development contract with each worker (see HMSO 1992: 141). This contract should spell out the expectations of both parties, the frequency, content, style and recording of the supervision. Amongst the advantages of a written contract is that the document can provide a reference point for both parties and that it can be used to address any conflict which may arise between the supervisor and the supervisee.

7.　The entire monitoring of the supervision programme should form part of the quality assurance process within the unit. It is important that all aspects of supervision are covered in this manner including individual and group supervision. The line manager and inspectors responsible for the unit should also ensure that supervision forms part of their quality assurance role. This external role provides a further check on the whole process and needs to be seen as having a positive contribution to the overall development of the supervision process.

8.　It is also important that the young people who live in the unit should be aware of, and informed about, the supervision process. Young people can easily feel that they are being excluded by the staff shutting themselves away for supervision. If however they understand something of the process, and that this is not a method for excluding them, then they are more likely to support the process. This might also contribute to reducing the incidence of interruption, which is an obvious threat to the supervision process in residential care. In explaining to young people what supervision is, parallels can be drawn with the experience of school; most young people will have experience of teachers taking them to one side to discuss their work with them. Effort needs to be put into explaining to young people the importance of the supervision process, remembering the definition of supervision that we have already given. It can also help young people understand why staff are in the building, but may not be available to undertake direct work with them.

Once the above structure is in place, it then should be possible to build on this to develop individual supervision programmes which are based on clarity of purpose and ownership of the process.

Individual supervision

All staff should receive individual supervision from their line manager. This includes those who are not employed as care staff but, by virtue of the fact that they work in a home, will come into contact with children. All staff will have emotional demands made upon them by the children; and will be obliged to respond. (The Children Act: Regulation and Guidance, Volume Four, 1.42, p. 10)

Supervision plays a 'vital role in maintaining standards and morale in Children's Homes' (HMSO 1992: 94). There is clearly a mandate for individual supervision to take place, a process, which as we have seen, is best facilitated within a supportive and well-resourced organisational framework. The use of an individual contract, developed together by the supervisor and the supervisee, will clarify expectations in relation to timing and frequency, the boundaries of confidentiality, content, style and recording of the supervision session. The Personal Development or Appraisal System should form the basis of the supervision process.

Let us examine how this would work in practice. If, for example, the supervision forum identified that the worker was unsure about their group work skills, together the supervisor and the supervisee would identify the steps to be taken to address this. These actions might include, for example:

- being paired with an experienced group worker in the team in order to facilitate direct learning
- engaging in training on a specific group work course
- studying relevant group work texts and theory and to use supervision as the forum to discuss how they relate to practice.

Once these actions have been followed through it is the task of the supervisor in the supervision sessions to monitor any progress. There needs to be clarity and honesty if these targets are to be met. This example has been chosen because of the centrality of group work skills to the residential task. A worker who, despite all the necessary educative and supportive inputs, is not able to develop their group work skills needs to be facilitated in helping to address this issue and reach a resolution that is consistent with the residential task and purpose.

Team supervision

Whilst team supervision cannot and should not replace individual supervision, it can be an exciting addition to it. The residential unit provides a setting which is complementary to a team approach to supervision:

> There is a difference between teams that share work with the same clients, such as a mental health team in a psychiatric hospital, or staff of a residential home, and teams which, although they work with similar approaches and in the same geographical area, have separate clients, such as a GP practice or a field social work team. (Hawkins and Shohet 1989: 12)

Thus it is the interdependence of the team which draws the distinction. An analogy is often drawn here with a sports team, where it is the overall cohesion of the team which is often the telling factor rather than individual 'star performances'. The residential child care team is similar: if communication is poor, or boundaries and roles are confused then the performance of the team as a whole will suffer.

It is important to draw the distinction between *team* and *group* supervision. Team supervision relates to the interdependence of the team members, joining together to share a common task of creating and sustaining a total living environment. In contrast group supervision brings together individuals who share similar work task but who do not necessarily work together. As Hawkins and Shohet (1989: 12) put it:

> It is important to recognise that team supervision is different from group supervision. It involves working with a group that has come together just for the purposes for joint supervision, but have an inter-related work life outside of the group.

Furthermore team supervision can be distinguished from group supervision as it contains an element of team development. Exactly how to organise and arrange team supervision will depend on the specifics of each unit, but the model adopted needs to be based in some fundamental considerations.

Group dynamics

Hawkins and Shohet write: 'We consider the team as an entity to be more than the sum of its parts and to have a personality and intra-psychic life of its own. This is termed by some writers as the team culture or team dynamic' (1989: 12).

A residential team manager will need to be aware of the dynamics and relationships within their particular team and will need to translate this awareness into practical strategies for working with the team. It is important that the residential manager works in ways which minimise the negative elements within the team dynamics.

The weekly team meetings create the opportunity for team supervision and development. Within the hectic life of a group living environment, these alone cannot sustain the need to address the dynamics of the team. It is helpful therefore to build a regular programme which involves team development days – these need to be about every four to six months. The needs of the team will vary according to the stage of development of the team (see Wiener 1992). Normally it is advisable for these days to be facilitated by an outside facilitator. The major hurdle which units have to jump to achieve these days is usually the difficult one of managing to get the full team together on any given day. One method which helps to address this is to make a reciprocal arrangement with another team so that units provide cover for each other's team development days.

Peer or paired supervision

Peer supervision can provide a useful adjunct to the supervision programme within a particular unit. Peer supervision involves practitioners organising themselves so that they receive supervision from one another. It can be argued that this is misnamed as it does not contain within it the managerial element of supervision – it may therefore be more helpful to see this as a form of consultancy, although the flow of consultancy will normally be in two directions. Such consultancy can be seen as positive and should be encouraged within units. Within the residential context there exists the opportunities to develop this way of working in ways that reflect the distinctiveness of the residential task. Normally, however, peer supervision or consultancy should be seen as an addition to the supervision programme within the unit and not a substitute for individual supervision.

In fact, peer consultancy forms an instrinsic part of the residential task. Two people working together on the same shift spend long periods working together. How they work together will influence practice within the unit significantly. They will be sharing decisions constantly, checking out decisions with one another and weighing up risks as a central aspect of good practice in residential care. Particularly important in working with young people is consistency, that is, to avoid one member of staff being seen as 'hard' and the other as 'soft'. In a sense then the realities of day-to-day practice involve us in informal aspects of consultancy.

Conclusion

In this chapter we have focused on the support and supervision of residential staff and suggested a variety of methods through which this can be addressed. We have argued that supervision is the cornerstone of a well-supported team. Supervision can also provide a supportive framework through which the residential task can become clarified and shared. It helps to mobilise the skills and resources to deliver the task and a method through which the achievement of tasks can be monitored. A well-organised and well-resourced supervisory programme can play an important role in supporting staff in the task of empowering children and young people.

7 The abuses and uses of residential child care[1]

Introduction

> 'I was beaten up until I started crying, then I was put on a social worker's knee and I would have to tell them the root of my problems.' (Young man remembering regression therapy, in his evidence to the Leicestershire Inquiry into the Frank Beck case)

> 'The social services took my son into care to rehabilitate him.' (His mother in Dorman 1992: 8)

How can we stop children being abused in care, those very same children who, ironically, are deemed by the authorities to have been abused or inadequately cared for by their own parents at home? It is this question which demands consideration in the context of this book as part of the process of helping to restore public and professional confidence in a system of substitute care which, as we demonstrated in Chapter 2, has never completely escaped from its Poor Law roots. Any model which aims to empower children and young people must address this fundamental abuse of power by adults over children. From the abuses at Kincora Boys' Home in East Belfast (Hughes 1985) to the Beeches Children's Home in Leicestershire (Kirkwood 1993) the contemporary connections, albeit unintended, with the 'less eligibility' theme are tragically obvious. During the last ten years, the abuse of children, including emotional, physical and sexual abuse, has been 'proven' in small and large

---

[1] This chapter draws on Mike Stein's presentation to an international conference 'Surviving Childhood Adversity', Trinity College, 2–5 July 1992 (Stein 1993).

children's homes, in assessment and treatment centres and in residential schools for children with physical disabilities and emotional and behavioural difficulties (HMSO 1991, 1992; Levy and Kahan 1991; Kirkwood 1993; Hughes 1985; Wescott and Clement 1992; Turk and Brown 1992). It is now evident from police investigations in many areas of England, Wales and Scotland that many – perhaps thousands – of young people were abused between the mid-1960s and the mid 1980s. But this does not suggest a new social phenomena: we know from the haunting accounts of older victims that many in the past must have suffered in silence (Doyle 1988; MacVeigh 1982). We also know that children are physically and sexually abused in foster care, and research from the United States suggests that children are nearly twice as likely to be abused in residential care than in their families (Pringle 1990, 1992; Nunno and Rindfleisch 1991).

In response to our initial question – how can we stop children being abused in care? – we would wish to pursue two lines of inquiry: first, a conceptual exploration of different forms of abuse in residential child care, and second, a consideration of the context in which abuse has arisen including, centrally, the low and marginal status of residential child care.

Conceptualising abuse

Since the mid-1980s there have been at least eight major independent inquiries into abuse in residential child care in the United Kingdom, and, in addition, four reviews, two surveys and a number of research studies into different aspects of residential child care. In general, the abuse inquiries have been set up following the conviction by a court of the perpetrator or, more unusually, following serious concern expressed at a public level, in respect of malpractice or problematic regimes. As these independent inquiries are almost exclusively legally chaired and led, disclosures of abuse have been defined by existing legislation and in the main divided into sexual offences or offences relating to physical harm and assault. The legal framework also identifies differing degrees or a tariff system of sexual and physical abuse. The Leeways Inquiry, for example, was set up following the conviction of an officer in charge of a children's home of various offences involving indecent photography of young children over a six-year period (Lawson 1985). And the Hughes Inquiry followed the conviction of six men for 49 offences including indecent assault, gross indecency and buggery against young people living at Kincora, an East Belfast Boys' Home (Hughes 1985). Two inquiries, the Leicestershire Inquiry and *Choosing with Care* (the Warner Report) (HMSO 1992), were set up following the conviction of Frank Beck, the officer in charge of three children's homes between 1973 and 1986, on seventeen counts involving both sexual and physical assault (HMSO 1992; Kirkwood 1993). His offences included buggery, rape and assault occasioning actual bodily harm.

However, not all inquiries have been in response to legal process. The Staffordshire Pindown Inquiry was set up in response to revelations of unacceptable practices in children's homes for exercising control over children by depriving them of their liberty and the Williams Inquiry on Ty Mawr Community Home in Wales was established following incidents of suicide and self-harm (Levy and Kahan 1991; Williams and Macreadie 1992).

The focus, by definition, and indeed the strength of these inquiries lies in their detailing and analysis of immediate events, including contexts, leading to abuse and in their practical recommendations, many of which have not been acted upon. However, there is a general failure to explore more critically and widely the concept of abuse in residential care.

Thinking conceptually about abuse suggests there are at least four different and distinctive forms – *sanctioned, institutional, systematic* and *individual* – themselves enveloped by wider structures of inequality, and therefore at the outset a crude homogeneity and an implicit standard or single response in addressing abuse in residential care must be discarded.

Sanctioned abuse

Susan was put into Pindown when she was nine years old: 'Susan admitted – very basic programme, be very nasty to her' (Log book entry). Susan was required to wear pyjamas and kept in a sparsely furnished room. She was not allowed contact with other children or non-Pindown staff and was not permitted to attend school. She was required to knock on the door before going to the toilet (Levy and Kahan 1991: 109).

> The hell started on the day I walked into the place. I had just left home and was naturally upset. I was quiet and tearful. Although I must have been there for a long time it just seemed like minutes later that they got hold of me. Accusing me of chucking out angry feelings, of hating my mother and sisters. When I tried to explain that I missed my mother they trapped me between their legs and dug their fingers into my ribs and made me scream and cry out in pain. This was what they called 'a temper tantrum'. They then put me into a wooden play pen. When I tried to get out Anne Daines got in and forcibly restrained me from getting out. When I finally gave in and stopped fighting I was allowed to get out and was given two chocolate bars for being 'a good girl' and doing things their way. This set the pattern for the next three years. We all got what they called treatment regularly, maybe three or four times a week. We didn't have to do anything. They just pounced on who they fancied. No excuse, just that they thought we were chucking out angry feelings. I would say most of us probably were. I mean we were being forced to use bottles

and being fed by a spoon. It was humiliating. We were dressed by staff and bathed by staff, male and female and generally degraded by them. We were angry and hurt. (Kirkwood 1993: 1)

The Staffordshire Pindown Report defined 'full' or 'total' Pindown as having the following features:

> Firstly, persistent isolation in a part of a children's home cordoned off as a special of Pindown unit; secondly removal of ordinary clothing for lengthy periods and the enforced wearing of shorts or night clothes; thirdly, persistent loss of all 'privileges'; fourthly, having to knock on the door to 'impart information'; for example, a wish to visit the bathroom; and fifthly, non-attendance at school, no writing or reading materials, no television, radio, cigarettes or visits. (Levy and Kahan 1991: 120)

There were variations of Pindown including 'Heavy Pindown', 'Strict Pindown', 'Negative Pindown', 'Nasty Pindown', 'B-plan Pindown', 'Stage 2 Pindown', 'Partial Pindown' and 'Therapeutic Pindown'. Pindown programmes were introduced in four Staffordshire children's homes at different times over just short of a six-year period during which time 132 children and young people were subjected to the regime. The principle architect of Pindown, Tony Latham, informed the Inquiry:

> ... the regime of Pindown which developed was based upon the principle that we were re-establishing control of the young person. By taking away all privileges from that person for a short period we felt that we would firstly force the young person to face up to his or her difficulties, and secondly provide the mechanism for negotiation with that person since by taking responsibility for their actions they could earn the privileges previously denied to them ... (Levy and Kahan 1991: 120)

One young person, Michael, who first went into Pindown when he was 11 years old, told the Inquiry:

> He was taken up to the back Pindown room and told to remove his clothes. He refused to do so. He was then held down on a bed in the room and stripped. He was made to have a bath and given a pair of pyjamas to wear. In addition to the bed the room contained a table and a chair. There were no reading or writing materials. He was not allowed to communicate with any other children. (Levy and Kahan 1991: 111)

Just as Tony Latham saw Pindown as a positive and effective form of intervention in young people's lives, there is little doubt from the voluminous evidence contained within the Leicestershire Inquiry report that Frank Beck possessed an evangelical belief in regression therapy and the creation of localised therapeutic communities (Kirkwood 1993). A qualified social worker, he was greatly influenced by his pre-course residential work experience which included regression, and by his reading of psychoanalytic works about child development and regression including Bettleheim, Erikson and Winnicott (see Kirkwood 1993: 60 and 133). The Leicestershire Inquiry report also highlighted the significance and influence of a film called *Warrendale* upon Beck's treatment methods. Members of the Inquiry viewed the film which Beck regularly showed to his care staff:

> In the course of the film, care staff appear to place heavy emphasis upon the value of ventilation of feelings, of 'getting out' from children their supposed deep seated feeling of anger and distress. That was achieved by deliberate oral and physical confrontation and provocation, physical restraint by one, two or more members of staff ('It's alright to be angry and it's especially alright to be angry when you are being held') and further goading until emotion was spent. In one of a number of episodes, the film portrays a male worker holding down a child and literally bellowing at her in confrontation and challenging and breaking down the child's defences. The 'successful' conclusion of such an episode was followed by a great deal of physical comforting and nursing of the child including washing, dressing, massaging, reading, cuddling and other attendance to children's needs. (Kirkwood 1993: 61)

The use of regression therapy in some of Leicestershire's children's homes and the so-called 'Pindown' system of control in operation in selected Staffordshire homes were in effect *sanctioned abuse* – which has also been referred to as 'programme abuse' (Gil 1982). We prefer the term 'sanctioned abuse' to capture the extent of legitimation of the programme by an authority. In addition, sanctioned abuse can also capture informal practices or cultures which can result in abuse. As forms of treatment they were not hidden or secret practices, but existed openly. The Staffordshire Pindown report contains the department's detailed documentation of different Pindown programmes, its underlying principles and its relationship to other departmental preventative and rehabilitative work including intermediate treatment (see Levy and Kahan 1990 Appendix F). The Leicestershire Inquiry report records in detail how Frank Beck gained widespread support for his treatment methods. During his 13-year period of employment this included active support by his two successive Directors of Social Service, by the Senior Managers of the 'Care Branch' responsible for his work, by field and residential workers and by three child psychiatrists. As with Pindown, there were documented 'treatment programmes' (see Kirkwood 1993: 82–5). And because he was so successful in gaining support for his treatment approach within the organisation, numerous complaints were responded to and defended by senior management as either a misunderstanding of his 'therapeutic' methods or symptoms of disturbed behaviour by young people. Frank Beck's work in Leicestershire was also nationally acclaimed, his work at the Beeches Children's Home being shown in an edition of a BBC Television programme *Brass Tacks* in August 1991 and written about in an article in *Community Care*, a national social work magazine, in January 1983. He also lectured widely and was a member of a Central Council for the Education and Training of Social Work (CCETSW) working party. It is perhaps not too difficult to understand such sanctioning without detailed scrutiny, for, although disowned and ridiculed with hindsight, both Beck's version of regression therapy rooted in psychoanalytic theory and Latham's Pindown regime derived from the rival behaviourist perspective seemed *at the time* to offer a solution to what was (and still is?) seen as an intractable problem: the care and, more pertinently, the control of some of the most difficult and disturbed young people in the care system. Senior and middle managers, field and residential social workers, the courts and the police, politicians and parents were all at one time or another desperate to find a solution to this problem without looking too closely or too critically at what was on offer, once the young person was 'no longer my responsibility'. Sanctioned abuse then suggests levels of collective responsibility not easily absolved by the imprisonment of a Frank Beck or the dismissal of a Tony Latham and such a recognition is also a pointer to the depth and extent of the challenge in preventing future abuse.

Also sanctioned abuse may not necessarily be underpinned by an explicit or embracing theoretical perspective and often includes extreme forms of everyday practices which become acceptable and therefore 'normal' in terms of the home's culture. Recent revelations from past practices in Sunderland Children's homes includes 'restraint' methods consisting of up to one hour of near-strangulation and a punishment system known as 'walking the gauntlet' which required young 'offenders' (that is, those who had broken home rules) stripped to the waist, to walk between two rows of staff and young people and be beaten by them according to their will. The careworker who reported these practices to senior managers described the children as being treated 'worse than animals'. And we know there are no easy solutions to be borrowed from elsewhere. The use of drugs to control young people in institutions in the United States for example is simply a different form of sanctioned abuse but more powerfully legitimised by the human sciences or what has been referred to as the 'psy complex' – medicine, psychiatry, psychology. (Foucault 1977a and b, 1979).

Institutional abuse

'When I leave care what will I know
Please help me now
Teach me how to grow'
(Young person still in care cited in Stein and Carey 1986: 151)

A second more substantial and pervasive form of abuse in residential child care is *institutional abuse*, which Gil (1982) refers to as system abuse. This is not to be confused or equated simply with institutionalisation but is of a similar conceptual order as institutional sexism or racism. Judged by outcomes, institutional abuse is the chronic failure of much residential child care (as well as other forms of substitute care), despite the commitment and caring of most of its largely untrained and poorly paid workforce, to be a compensatory parent particularly to those young people estranged from their own families who need preparation and support in their transition to adulthood. A growing body of research, powerfully amplified by the voices of young people themselves, shows how substitute care generally fails to compensate and assist them developmentally, emotionally and educationally, so that by the time they leave care their life chances are very poor indeed. The largest study of placement patterns yet completed suggested a social work defined success rate of about one-third for residential care placements with the aim of independence (Rowe et al. 1989). We also know from recent research studies that care leavers are likely to have experienced movement and disruption whilst in care, as well as problems of identity stemming from separation and a lack of knowledge of their past (which may be amplified for black and mixed parentage young people brought up in a predominantly 'white' care system), social isolation and a weakening of family links, poor educational performance, stigma and too little preparation for leaving (see Stein, 1997).

On leaving care at between 16 and 18 years of age, paradoxically far younger than 'non-care' young people leave home, loneliness, isolation, unemployment, poverty, homelessness, movement and 'drift' are likely to feature significantly in many of their lives. Young women in care are far more likely to become parents at a younger age, that is under 18, than their non-care counterparts and recent research also confirms high levels of unemployment, dependence on income support and social services financial assistance for care leavers (Stein and Carey 1986; Stein 1990; Biehal et al. 1995; Garnett 1992). A number of studies have suggested that about one-third of the young homeless have been 'in care' (Streetwise National Coalition 1991). Two surveys by Centrepoint, based upon its London night shelter, suggest that this percentage increased from 34 per cent in 1987 to 57 per cent in 1989, including young people who had lived in children's homes and foster care (Randall 1988, 1989). And when care leavers become homeless they are exposed to danger – from ill-health, crime and prostitution. The latest Centrepoint survey found that a third of its young residents had been approached to become involved in prostitution since coming to London. There is also disturbing evidence from two very small-scale studies that a high proportion of beggars (50 per cent) and male prostitutes (66 per cent) had experience of local authority care and a number of studies have demonstrated a strong correlation between care and offending including custodial disposals (Stockley 1990).

This is not in any way to suggest, simplistically, that care is the *cause* of their problems which may be deeply rooted within past family difficulties including damaging and abusive relationships, or, crudely, that they would have been *better off* if left or returned home as if that were a chosen or realistic option. Nor is it, naively, to fall into the trap of juxtaposing the 'bad' residential care option with the 'good' fostering option – as foster home breakdown rates and unsuccessful outcomes for this age group are similar to residential care and as many young people's care careers include both foster and residential care (Rowe et al. 1989). Also we know there are good examples of residential care as well as foster care (Social Services Inspectorate 1991). Neither is it to ignore the impact of major changes in social legislation and the under-resourcing of public services. This includes the restructuring of social security (by the abolition of income support for 16- and 17-year-olds and the ending of householder status for under 25 year olds) based on the duel assumptions of 'family responsibility' and the availability of youth training places – both problematic for care leavers (NACAB 1992; SSAC 1992; Stein 1990). What is being suggested, supported by our existing knowledge, is that the care system, including residential child care, generally fails to compensate and assist many of these young people. However, simply identifying institutional abuse from problematic outcomes is not very helpful in terms of generating a response. We need a working definition.

Institutional abuse can be defined as the policies, procedures and practices which create or contribute towards problems of instability, dependency, stigma, identity formation and under-achievement, the major problem areas highlighted by recent research studies. Against a background of diverse needs, it is difficult to suggest priorities but the failure of our system of substitute care to offer many young people stability, that very stability which was often judged to be missing in their own families and backgrounds, raises fundamental questions about the rationale of the system itself. We know from a number of studies that most long-term young people in care experience multiple placements but such an objective description as 'multiple placements' cannot capture the emotional impact upon young people of changing carers, friends, neighbourhoods, schools, on several occasions, with little constancy in their lives. Neither, despite the resilience of young people, can it capture the emotional energy and strength required by these young people to meet changing expectations derived from new relationships and different social situations – those very same young people whose own developmental stages have often been impaired or damaged by their pre-care experiences. A rare convergence of sociological, psychological and psychiatric perspectives would conceive being in care, under these conditions, as an assault on personal identity. Providing stability for young people is prioritised as a prerequisite for addressing the related areas of dependency, stigma, identity and under-achievement. But this is not in any way to downgrade the significance of these dimensions in their own right. They are too important. Dependency and stigma, as forms of institutional abuse include, for example, policies, procedures and practices from a 'bulk-buying' economy and the denial of personal privacy to the lack of involvement and participation by young people in decision making. And similarly, identity problems may result from a failure to assist young people in gaining essential knowledge and understanding of cultural, ethnic and family roots and separation. And again, under-achievement may be connected to a range of institutional care policies and practices including lack of privacy, low carer expectations and poor school links.

Systematic and individual abuse

'He did not complain to anyone about the homosexual activities of the warden and assistant warden and told us there was nobody to whom to complain ... he said that he was ashamed of this relationship and feared that he himself might be in trouble if he reported it to the police.' (Resident of Kincora Boys Home, cited by Pinkerton and Kelly 1986: 23)

'As far as I am concerned, Kincora was a vital facility which I used as a social worker and which I recommended others to use ...' (Interview with social worker, Belfast (Smythe 1991: 141)

A third form of abuse in residential care is *systematic abuse* which can be defined as the organised emotional, physical or sexual abuse (or some combination of these) of numbers of children and young people in care by members of staff, or other adults, over a period of time. Evidence is emerging that this may include organised paedophile activity (HMSO 1997). In contrast to sanctioned abuse it is not directly linked to a defined treatment philosophy or cultural practice. For example, from as early as 1967 some boys at the Kincora Boys' Home in East Belfast made written complaints of homosexual advances (although many did not, such as the resident cited above); these reports continued to be unheard until 1980 when, following widespread media interest, three members of staff and three other men were convicted and sentenced of 49 offences including buggery, gross indecency and indecent assault (Hughes 1985).

Systematic abuse can be distinguished from a fourth abuse form, *individual abuse*, most usually involving a single member of staff abusing one or more young persons physically or sexually (or both) and of which many such cases are recorded in the history of residential care including private and public schools.

Societal inequalities

Recognition of these different forms of abuse – sanctioned, institutional, systematic and individual – is an important starting point in addressing the question of prevention but before moving on there also needs to be recognition of the way wider societal inequalities of power envelope abuse in residential child care. The most significant commonalities are *gender* and *generation* – the abuse of children by adults, most frequently (although not exclusively) male adults.

Given the high levels of childhood sexual abuse recorded in both the United States and the United Kingdom (recent research suggests rates of one in four for females and one in six for males in the United States and as high as one in two for females and one in four for males in the United Kingdom (Finklehor et al. 1990; Kelly 1991)) it is perhaps not surprising that this is reflected to some extent in both residential and foster care. Sexually abusing males predominate and, as feminist writers have suggested, we cannot ignore the contemporary construction of masculinity (in terms of the spectrum or continuum of abuse – from routine dominance onwards to rape and violence) and structures of patriarchy in the genesis of sexual abuse (Kelly 1989; Violence Against Children Study Group 1990). But neither should we ignore *generation* although it is rarely conceptualised as a comparable indicator of inequality as gender or indeed ethnicity or social class. And yet it is very difficult to make sense of the experiences of children and young people without recognising the construction of childhood as a period of dependency and powerlessness and without perceiving children and young people as an identifiable social group with their own set of interests (Frost and Stein 1989; Jenks 1996).

In relation to abuse in residential care, we need to understand the complex interaction of different indicators of powerlessness including the direct exploitative relationships between mainly *male adults* and *children* in sanctioned, systematic and individual forms of physical and sexual abuse and, more subtly and indirectly, through disempowering structures, policies and practices in institutional abuse. These include the interaction of gender and generation in reinforcing 'traditional' gender divisions, domestic roles, education and career paths, behavioural expectations; the interaction of generation and institutional racism – by the under-representation of black staff as black role models, and the neglect of cultural knowledge and identity issues.

The structures of abuse discussed are illustrated below (in Figure 7.1).

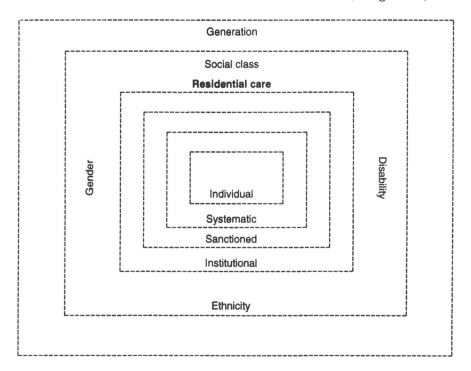

Figure 7.1   **Conceptualising abuse: societal inequalities and abuse in residential child care**

Note: (i) size of the boxes suggests the relative status of different dimensions – e.g. institutional abuse is a larger-scale problem than individual abuse
(ii) The broken lines allow for interaction between different dimensions.

Source: Stein 1993: 240.

Conclusion

How do we account for substitute care becoming in part substitute abuse, that is, a publicly and professionally perceived 'solution' becoming part of the 'problem'?

The general historical context, including the shift from residential to community care, we have already discussed in our historical chapter. From the early 1960s onwards, a political consensus underpinned initially by cost-cutting economics and increasingly by the idealisation of 'the family' and 'community' combined with a rare academic unity of assault on institutions: sociology, social policy, politics, psychiatry and psychology all generated what were considered seminal critiques of institutional life (Dalley 1988; Senior 1989).

More specifically in relation to residential child care permanency planning for substitute family care, including more directed adoption and fostering policies and practices, boosted by 'selective' negative aspects of state care (for example, by focusing upon criticisms of residential child care and downplaying foster care breakdowns) identified in a series of research studies published during the 1970s and 1980s, led to a loss of faith in the residential child care option (Cliffe and Berridge 1991). The impact of these changes in terms of the philosophy, purpose, staffing and morale in residential child care has been devastating. In general, the staff who have the most contact with children and young people have the least training and experience. Moreover child care workers are often left overstressed, isolated, with inadequate support, the very conditions which have been linked to abusing parents (Nunno and Rindfleisch 1991). Residential child care has generally been operating in a climate of denial and welfare planning blight as well as in a theoretical void. It is perhaps not surprising that peddlers of half-baked psychotherapy and crude behaviourism would be listened to and the door left open.

An analysis of recent abuse inquiries (Berridge and Brodie 1998) has identified a number of common themes relating to the key managerial, policy and practice issues which we have explored throughout this book:

> These include inadequate line management; minimum direct management contact with children and staff; unsatisfactory placement policies and processes; inadequate recruitment processes and staff training; reluctance to use secure provision and more specialised alternatives; inadequate or no external expert advice; and lest we should overlook the rather obvious fact that most of these scandals are committed directly by men, the presence of 'macho' or masculine charisma or culture. (11: 1998)

How we address these issues and help to create a positive alternative will be addressed in our concluding chapter.

8   Leaving residential care

Introduction

The major contribution of residential care to the accommodation, preparation and after-care of teenagers is confirmed by recent research and government information. Research studies examining care careers have highlighted the key accommodation role for this age group (Rowe et al. 1989; Stone 1990; Cliffe and Berridge 1992) and the significance of residential care as the last placement for a majority of all care leavers (Biehal et al. 1992). As many as two-thirds of care leavers, aged 16–18, are likely to have lived in residential care at some time during their care career and over half are likely to leave care from a residential placement. During the most recent year for which government information is available similar proportions 'ceased to be looked after' from foster and residential care – that is, despite the intense public and professional scrutiny of residential care and the reported transfer of resources to foster care in recent years (HMSO 1991; Cliffe and Berridge 1992; Stein 1993; DOH 1995).

The experiences of young people leaving residential care has also been central to 'the awakening of leaving care in the professional and political consciousness' (Stein 1991). For it was the Who Cares? project that, between 1977 and 1979, brought together young people living in children's homes in different parts of the country to talk about their lives in care. A common theme emerging from their voices was the lack of power over their lives, for example, in having to use order books instead of money to buy clothes, in not being able to attend their reviews, in their limited opportunities to shop, cook and, more generally, to participate in the decisions which shaped their lives. And the dependency created by care was linked to their fears about reaching 18 and leaving care:

> 'In my home you don't have to do anything. Your cooking's done, your washing's done, everything is done ...that's what I mean. I'm not prepared for it. I don't know how I will manage, I can't even boil an egg.'

> 'They plan your life for you ... and then all of a sudden say "good-bye".'

The Who Cares? project led to the setting up of local in care groups in different parts of the UK and in 1979 to its successor organisation, the National Association of Young People in Care (NAYPIC). They campaigned actively to improve conditions for care leavers culminating in their evidence to the House of Commons Social Services Committee in 1984 in which they stressed the need for: 'Greater preparation whilst in care, resources made available when you are leaving and the continued help and support of someone who you know will be around and whom you can trust' (Sharing Care, NAYPIC 1983).

Like Who Cares?, its predecessor, NAYPIC's membership was primarily drawn from young people living in children's homes and it was the connections between their lives in care and their lives after leaving which informed much of their campaigning work and which led to increased public awareness.

Also, from the mid-1970s, findings from research studies, in the main derived from the experiences of young people leaving residential care, highlighted the many problems they faced thus echoing the voices from Who Cares?, NAYPIC, Black and In Care and local in care groups (Godek 1976; Klein 1985; Stein and Maynard 1985; Stein and Carey 1986; First Key 1987).

During the 1980s campaigning groups and organisations such as Centrepoint, First Key and Barnardos publicised the plight of homeless care leavers, particularly drawing attention to the over-representation of those who had lived in children's homes, and the impact of changes in benefit entitlement upon their lives (Randall 1988, 1989; Stein 1990).

It was against this background that the 'Continuing Care' recommendations of the 1984 Social Services Committee Report on Children in Care were framed and subsequently amended culminating in the new duties and wider discretionary powers in respect of 'leaving care' contained within the Children Act 1989: duties to prepare young people for leaving care (section 24.1) and to advise and befriend young people to the age of 21, where they left care after their 16th birthday (section 24.2); discretionary powers to offer financial assistance to young people in relation to housing, education, employment or training (sections 24.6.1 and 24.8). It was also against this background that there has been a growth of different policy and practice initiatives at the local level developed in response to the problems experienced by care leavers.

In this chapter we will begin by exploring, from a research perspective, care leavers' experiences of 'being looked after' with a particular focus on residential care. We will then consider their lives after-care including the contribution of different leaving care schemes and approaches.

Being looked after

Movement and disruption

The largest survey of care leavers (aged 16–18) to date indicated that the last placement for over half of the young people was in the residential sector including children's homes, independence units, assessment centres and community homes with education (Biehal et al. 1995). Consistent with the findings of other studies, most of these young people entered care as teenagers and experienced a high degree of movement and disruption during the time they were 'looked after'. In one study, fewer than one in ten of the young people remained in the same placement and nearly a third made between four and nine moves; a small number of young people moved more than ten times (Biehal et al. 1995). And in another study, half of the young people being assisted by a leaving care scheme had between six and twelve placements by the time they were 16 years of age (Stein 1990). Placement moves can, of course, be planned and lead to positive outcomes but many are as a result of breakdowns and are often experienced by young people as another relationship failure and rejection, followed by a changing social world – having to get to know new residential care staff and friends, a different neighbourhood and sometimes a new school. The extent and experience of such change is a very distinguishing feature of being 'looked after' compared with the lives of 'non-care' young people (Stein and Carey 1986).

Identities

For young people who have experienced several moves and those separated from their families for many years – two-thirds for more than three years and two-fifths for more than ten years (Biehal et al. 1995) – issues of identity, of having a 'story' of their lives, including knowledge of their past and present, must be addressed. For some young people life-story books have helped, but for others: 'their experiences and relationships were too complex, disrupted or painful to be easily transformed into a single linear narrative' (Biehal et al. 1995).

More than just factual knowledge was required, by helping young people not only to understand – avoiding the superficiality of authorised versions or simple lists of events – but to come to terms with this knowledge, for example, by making sense of their parents' rejection of them, and of the ensuing events in their lives. The same research study also captured the subtle and complex views of ethnic identity held by black and mixed-heritage young people. For these young people, as their circumstances changed, as relationships with families or close friends developed or were ended, their views about their ethnic origins changed and their sense of ethnic identity was subtly transformed, although some social workers still held to more fixed biological or cultural 'racial' identities.

Self-care

An important part of preparation for leaving residential care is the acquisition of self-care skills. By this we mean five main areas: budgeting skills including shopping and managing finances; decision making and negotiation skills; practical skills such as cooking, cleaning and maintaining accommodation; diet and personal hygiene, and sex education. For most young people the acquisition of these life skills is a gradual process beginning in childhood and progressing with increasing age and development. It is also a supported and holistic process usually taking place in the context of close and stable family relationships. And it is a participatory process involving family discussions, negotiations, risk taking, making mistakes and trying again.

A common theme arising out of the earlier literature on residential care has been the 'dominant guidance' and the lack of opportunities for young people in children's homes to participate in the decisions which affect their lives, including important self-care areas. Using vouchers and order books to buy clothes, central purchasing of food, bulk buying of toiletries, fixed menus, a failure to address the specific needs of black young people and a general lack of consultation and discussion of key life-stage issues have all been identified as undesirable policies and practices in the care system (First Key 1987; Black and in Care 1984; Denton 1984; Stein 1983; Stein and Ellis 1983; Page and Clarke 1977). In highlighting the insensitivity of the 'independence philosophy' to the young person's psycho-social development, Stein and Carey (1986) drew attention to the 'domestic combat courses' of independence units where young people were marked out of ten on a checklist for each activity, from opening a tin of baked beans to folding sheets and then 'passing out' when they have reached the required standard.

A study of leaving care schemes, *Moving On* which explores in depth the experiences of 74 young people over a two-year period sheds more light on the acquisition of self-care skills (Biehal et al. 1995). The research found that some of the young people in residential care had positive experiences, particularly where they were encouraged and supported by staff to do their own cooking, shopping, handle their own money and look after themselves, in short, to participate in the care process. However the size and culture of some children's homes is such that preparation was seen as appropriate only when the young person moved to a semi-independence unit. And thus, far from being a gradual and holistic process, preparation became a crash course in practical skills, neglecting the young person's emotional development, which is just as important for their successful adjustment after care.

The *Moving On* research also found little systematic planning within residential care to deal with issues around sexual relationships and health, leaving young people to find out what they could from school and friends and sometimes their social worker.

The evidence from *Moving On* also suggests that the cultural self-care needs of black young people are not always met, particularly opportunities to learn and practice different styles of cooking and carers' ignorance of special hair and skin care needs. The research also found that young women both acquired and maintained self-care skills far more than young men including practical skills, especially managing money, and negotiating skills. This suggests the need to tackle gender-related assumptions amongst boys – and residential carers – at an early stage in their careers.

Moving on from care

Transitions and accommodation

Research completed during the last ten years has shown that young people continue to leave care at a much earlier age than other young people leave home (Stein and Carey 1986; Biehal et al. 1995; Stein 1997). In *Moving On* (Biehal et al. 1995), nearly two-thirds of the young people left before they were 18 and a quarter did so at just 16. Some of these young people's residential and foster placements broke down, precipitating a rapid move out of care. But for others, particularly those from children's homes, there was too often the assumption that they should move on having reached 16 or 17 years of age. Just under half of the group moved to transitional forms of accommodation such as lodgings and stays with friends. And for some of these young people who were not yet ready for independent accommodation this proved to be helpful preparation. A fifth (20 per cent) moved to independent tenancies in the public, voluntary or private sector when they first left care and this figure rose to around 60 per cent 18–24 months later. Most of these young people needed ongoing support to sustain their tenancies but lack of preparation, coping with new freedoms and loneliness led to some losing or leaving their tenancies. For many of these young people, their first two years out of care were marred by movement and instability, with over half making two or more moves and a sixth making five or more moves. Just over one-fifth became homeless at some stage.

Specialist leaving care schemes played a major part in this 'moving on' process, particularly in assisting young people leaving residential care. Their work included planning transitions, preparing young people (sometimes compensating them for what they had lacked in preparation in their children's homes), providing follow-up support and meeting accommodation needs. In relation to accommodation, specialist schemes between them were offering directly managed accommodation in trainer flats or specialist hostels, floating support schemes, arranging access to supported lodgings or hostels provided by other agencies and supporting young people in independent tenancies. Even for those young people experiencing the greatest instability, continuity of support by the schemes often prevented a descent into homelessness or a rapid escape from it. In *Moving On* the analysis of accommodation outcomes showed that not only were specialist schemes working with those who had the most unstable housing careers but also that they were able to help the vast majority of young people find good accommodation within two years.

Education and career patterns

Another consistent finding during the last ten years has been the low educational attainment of care leavers and the failure of care to compensate young people for their damaging pre-care experiences and thus establish a successful pattern of schooling (Stein and Carey 1986; Biehal et al. 1992, 1995; Stein 1994). The evidence suggests significantly lower attainment levels and post-16 participation levels compared to non-care young people (Banks et al. 1992; Stein 1994). Movement and disruption in care, labelling, residential carers' low expectations, lack of private study space and a negative educational culture in children's homes, prioritising 'welfare' over educational concerns and truancy and school exclusion may all contribute to a history of poor schooling and thus jeopardise future careers on leaving (Stein 1994). In *Moving On* half the young people were unemployed within a few months of leaving care and nearly two-thirds of them failed to establish a stable career pattern, facing periods of short-term casual work interspersed with episodes of training and unemployment. As a result most of the young people were poor, living on or near benefit levels. The specialist schemes all played a central role in administering finance for young people and, to varying degrees, in developing and co-ordinating policies including helping social services discharge their discretionary powers to offer financial assistance under Section 24 of the Children Act 1989. However, the developmental role of schemes in promoting education, training and employment was less developed than in other areas of their work, that is beyond their work with individual care leavers.

Identities and networks

The significance of identity for 'looked after' young people has already been referred to. It is often at the point of leaving care that many young people attempt to make sense of their past, to trace missing relatives, to find continuity in their lives and a sense of belonging. They need a 'story' of their lives that makes sense to reduce their confusion about both how and why events had happened as they did and thus provide a more secure platform for their futures in the adult world. Research suggests that those young people who retained their family links, even where contact was not very positive, seemed better able to do this. Knowledge of their families, at a minimum, gave a greater symbolic certainty to their lives. Those who remained confused about their past found life out of care more difficult to manage: they lacked self-esteem, were less confident and assertive. *Moving On* suggests there was little perceived difference between black and mixed-heritage young people and white young people in relation to their degree of self-esteem, knowledge of their background and general sense of purpose. Indeed the black young people were slightly more likely to have a secure sense of identity, in these terms, than the white young people. As suggested earlier, for these young people their sense of ethnic identity changed over time and their identification with a particular group was strongly related to their identification or rejection of family members.

Moving On, consistent with the findings of other studies (Bullock et al. 1993) has highlighted the importance of family links – including contact with brothers and sisters, grandparents and other members of their extended family – while recognising poor family relationships often ruled out a return home. The same study also revealed that half of the young women in the sample had become parents themselves, half of the pregnancies being unplanned, a third planned with partners, and three-quarters of parents living with their partners at some stage. The specialist schemes played only a minimal role in mediating between young people and their families, tending to view this as the social worker's responsibility. But this was not always the case, for fewer than one-third of social workers were active in this area once the young person had moved on. When social workers became involved with young parents, whether as a result of child care concerns or not, there was a pervasive tendency to focus on monitoring child care and thus switch their support from mother to child. In contrast, the specialist schemes, when involved, were able to support the mother in her own right. The schemes were also active in helping young people develop friendship networks. Their specialist knowledge of local youth and leisure provision as well as their own groups and drop-in arrangements were highly valued by young people.

A secure sense of identity is the emotional platform for leaving care. In *Moving On* those young people with a secure sense of identity had good social networks and relationship skills, whereas many of those with an insecure sense of identity had poor social networks and relationship skills. And most of the young people with a secure sense of identity had positive family links.

Conclusion

As we have argued, residential care makes a major contribution to the lives of teenagers preparing to move on to the adult world. Recent research points to the need for more placement stability and less movement and disruption, including challenges to practices and policies which create pressure for young people to move before they are ready to do so. Young people need to be given opportunities to explore their personal histories, but this cannot be a one-off purely factual exercise – many young people want ongoing and skilled help to construct and refine their 'stories'. The acquisition of self-care skills are essential to preparing young people for adult life, and for young people in residential care, as for all young people, the process should be gradual, supported, participatory and holistic. Particular attention should be paid to the self-care needs of black and mixed-heritage young people, and in challenging gender-related assumptions. Past educational deficits cast a long shadow over the career opportunities of most care leavers and raise important issues about stability, prioritisation, compensation and strategies to promote a more positive culture of educational achievement in children's homes. Specialist leaving care teams can make a substantial contribution in achieving positive accommodation outcomes and in providing ongoing support services and networks for residential care leavers. But they can only build upon what has gone before – good-quality residential child care. In our final chapter we will examine how we can move forward to this.

9   A future for residential child care?

Introduction

In this book we have examined the current state of residential care, drawing on history, theory, law, research and practice experience. This analysis provides a foundation for proposing practice and policy directions for the future of residential child care. We have argued that while residential child care has faced a series of crises, it is possible to re-create residential child care as a positive alternative. In this conclusion we aim to bring together the implications of this book and thereby suggest a tentative blueprint for ensuring the quality of future residential child care.

The way forward?

The case needs to be made for a positive role of residential child care. Here we agree with Sir William Utting (HMSO 1991a, 1997) that it is possible, despite the various problems it has faced, for residential child care to be a positive and creative resource in the future. For this to become a reality however certain factors need to be in place.

First, an issue which has emerged throughout this book, and which is confirmed by recent research findings (Sinclair and Gibbs forthcoming), is that high-quality residential child care can only happen where there is a clear and well-defined purpose for each residential unit. The introduction of the Statement of Purpose for each unit has been a major step forward in this area. In theory, at least, each unit should now have a clear written statement outlining what this purpose is and how it will be achieved. We know, however, that many managers and residential workers are frustrated that the often fine promises in these statements are difficult to deliver. The Statements can be undermined by a lack of resources, changes within and outside of the unit, and lack of ownership, either by the staff team or the organisation more widely. These problems should not be allowed to undermine the principle of the Statement of Purpose, which forms the basis for quality in residential child care.

Second, we have argued that the effectiveness of residential care units is enhanced where they are small – perhaps providing around six places. This has a number of advantages:

- It helps avoid tendencies towards institutional practices
- It encourages a caring environment, with individualised care
- It facilitates communication and a sense of ownership amongst both staff and young people
- It helps to avoid the behavioural problems which can emerge from large groups of young people living in one unit.

Third, again as Utting (HMSO 1997) has emphasised, quality residential child care needs to be seen as part of a wider system of provision for children and young people. Utting has expressed his concern that the sector has declined to such an extent that the possibility of real choice for young people is in danger of being undermined. Quality residential child care needs to be seen as part of a system to offer real choice at all stages. This means that services need to be strategically planned to include family support, child protection and services for children living apart from their parents. All parts of the system need to communicate and be aware of how they impact on each other. They need to plan, work and communicate together.

Fourth, and following from this, a sound residential system needs to run alongside a child care system which is based on support and prevention. It has been demonstrated that, for example, well-planned and organised prevention and support teams, working with the 'older' young people who are likely to be placed in residential establishments can be effective (see Frost 1997, for example). These teams can help to ensure that residential placements are used effectively and efficiently and not simply because there is no realistic alternative.

Our vision would be of young people's support teams at the pivotal point of a system which linked preventive interventions with young people and their families, and different forms of substitute care, including foster and residential care. This would be an integrated and flexible system emphasising links both *within* different forms of substitute care and *between* prevention, support and substitute care. This system would need to be facilitated by a greater visibility and an increased awareness of costs and outcomes. The former would be achieved through decentralised budgets managed by the young people's support teams thus relating costs of residential care – currently estimated at £61,000 per year (see Sinclair and Gibbs forthcoming) – to those of the other services:

> Social services spend approximately two and a half times as much on residential care as they do on disabled children and those on the child protection register put together. Taken as a whole the sector costs nearly 50% more than foster care which provides roughly six times as many placements. (Sinclair and Gibbs forthcoming)

The second part of the equation would require the further refinement and development of the *Looking After Children* materials so that they can be used with children and young people when and wherever they are receiving social work services, including prevention and support – not just when they are being 'looked after' as at present. In addition to facilitating individual care plans these materials have the potential to deliver aggregate data in starting points and outcomes which can then be linked to costs. This would provide the basis of a more strategic approach to responding to needs and providing services.

As we have suggested earlier in this book, the Statement of Purpose is to be welcomed as a useful planning tool. This could be developed to be applicable to different forms of foster and residential care. The determining factor should be to provide the best possible placement to meet the assessed needs of the child or young person: to achieve this will require far more closely integrated systems than exist at the moment. The aim and purpose of each form of substitute care should be regularly reviewed. We thus see the idea of clarifying the purpose of each form of care as a dynamic and holistic process – and we would be sceptical of a return to the rigid system of classification of care that existed in the past. This system – which specified residential care as Community Home (Education), assessment centres and so on – was produced by a dynamic of size, geographical distance and labelling of young people. We envisage the new approach as providing more enabling and individualised group care in small homes – whether that is residential or foster care – and thus embracing the wide range of socialisation roles that we take for granted in households, but with additional support and therapeutic services purchased or provided by the young people support teams.

There is no doubt that within this system we need high-quality secure accommodation – not least to resist the drift towards more punitive forms of provision such as Secure Training Centres. This does not mean however that we require a move towards more specialisation and, implicit within this, more geographical distance as some recent commentators have suggested (HMSO 1997; Sinclair and Gibbs forthcoming). The lessons of past abuse, the ease of contemporary communication, the need to develop integrated prevention at community level, the importance of family links and the high percentage of young people who return home, all suggest that small, localised units have much to offer.

Fifth, as we have suggested throughout this book, empowerment offers a concept which can inform the development of residential child care. Empowerment suggests a model which can move beyond previous paternalistic models of 'care' and more recent, and sometimes, naive models based solely on the rights of children. The empowerment model can work on three levels: those of the individual, the group and the citizen.

At the individual level, empowerment suggests that each child and young person can be supported in achieving more control, having more power, over their own lives. Empowerment is a powerful concept which suggests that children and young people should be supported in a manner which enables them to take risks and take control over their own lives wherever this is possible and as long as it promotes their welfare in the long term. Empowerment here needs to be distinguished from children's participatory rights. In certain circumstances a child may claim a right, for example, to stay out late at night, which may be denied within an empowerment model. The residential worker might feel, based on an assessment of the risks, that by allowing the young person to stay out late at night that the young person will be at risk, say, of sexual exploitation. It is clear therefore that empowerment and children's rights need to be distinguished.

Our model of empowerment also recognises at the individual level the differing ways in which children and young people who enter substitute care are initially disempowered – for example, through their experiences of physical, sexual, emotional abuse or neglect – and thus present as troubled or troublesome young people. Our proposed young people support teams would play a key role in assessing such needs and ensuring that specialist services are available to young people and their carers.

The group is the defining aspect of residential child care – such care is an experience of group living. The group offers a powerful vehicle for empowerment. It helps us learn to live in social situations and to make the compromises that are often implied by such living. The group can also be a powerful forum for decision making. The empowerment model suggests that the group can be focus for much effective decision making. Young people in group care settings can be involved in many of the decisions which we have examined in this study, ranging from issues relating to their diet to staff selection, from decor to unit rules.

At the citizen level, it is important to note that we all form a part of larger social groupings – what we might call communities of interest. In this context we are referring to collective organisations of young people in care. This group, although like many communities, sometimes divided by factors such as gender, race or ability, can be a powerful group which has much to gain from acting in a shared setting. Sir William Utting has argued persuasively that young people in care need to be collectively represented in order to ensure that they are safeguarded: 'It is important that those who are or who have been in local authority care should be represented by bodies which not only act as advocates but also contribute to the development of policy and practice directly' (HMSO 1997: 112).

Such collective organisation will enable young people to be empowered to influence policy and practice at a macro level, that is, to have a voice and campaign on all pertinent issues in relation to the provision for young people in care.

Summary

In summary, empowerment has a number of advantages as a theoretical and practice framework. It allows us to understand and engage wider societal inequalities including gender, ethnicity, disability and, crucially, generation – the powerlessness derived from the status of childhood and youth – and their impact upon residential care. As suggested earlier this points to an exploration of the interaction of one or more of these dimensions of inequality with generation, in terms of their implications for residential care policy and practice: thinking about, for example, the staff composition (including gender and ethnic make-up) and the practice of role modelling for young women who have been sexually abused or black and mixed-parentage young people living in care; thinking about, for example, group care-practice with able-bodied young people and those with special needs in preparing them together for adulthood. Empowerment, then, has the potential to inform a practice framework, complimentary to the legal framework contained within the Children Act 1989, to guide both policy and practice. But, ideally, more than that, empowerment can restore belief in residential child care, thus furthering a practice based upon engagement, negotiation and participation, a practice which may utilise different methods and approaches but not be a slave to them, being guided by the question 'How will this empower the young person?' And, finally, empowerment can bring about a practice which will not be polarised between a shallow and token legalism which rejects all *needs* in favour of *rights* or conversely a crude and narrow pathologising which reduces young people to a receptacle of professionally defined needs.

Bibliography

Audit Commission (1994) *Seen But Not Heard* (London: HMSO).

Baldwin, N. (1989) *The Power to Care in Children's Homes* (London: Avebury).

Banks, M., Bates, I., Breakwell, G., Bynner, J., Emler, N., Jamieson, L. and Roberts, K. (1992) *Careers and Identities* (Buckingham: Open University Press).

Bebbington, A. and Miles, J. (1989) 'The background of children who enter local authority care', *British Journal of Social Work*, Vol. 19, No. 5, pp. 349–68.

Berridge, D. (1985) *Children's Homes* (Oxford: Blackwell).

Berridge, D. and Cleaver, H. (1987) *Foster Home Breakdown* (Oxford: Blackwell).

Berridge, D. (1994) 'Foster and residential care reassessed: a research perspective', *Children and Society*, Volume 8, Number 2.

Berridge, D. and Brodie, I. (1998) *Children's Homes Revisited* (London: Jessica Kingsley).

Biehal, N., Clayden, J., Stein, M. and Wade, J. (1992) *Prepared for Living? A survey of young people leaving the care of three local authorities* (London: National Children's Bureau).

Biehal, N., Clayden, J., Stein, M. and Wade, J. (1995) *Moving On* (London: HMSO).

Black and in Care (1984) *Black and in Care Conference Report* (London: Children's Legal Centre).

British Association of Counselling (1987) *Code of Ethics* (London: BAC).

Bruce, M., (1968) *The Coming of the Welfare State* (London: Batsford).

Bullock, R., Little, M. and Millham, S. (1993) *Going Home* (Aldershot: Dartmouth).

Cale, M., (1993) 'Girls and the Perception of Sexual Danger in the Victorian Reformatory System', *History*: 201–17.

Campbell, B. (1993) *Goliath: Britain's Dangerous Places* (London: Methuen).

Clayden, J. and Stein, M. (1996) 'Self Care Skills and Becoming Adult', in Department of Health (ed.), *Looking After Children Reader* (London: HMSO).

Clegg, S. (1989) *Frameworks of Power* (London: Sage).

Cliffe, D. and Berridge, D. (1991) *Closing Children's Homes: An End to Residential Care?* (London: National Children's Bureau).

Cohen, S. (1985) *Visions of Social Control* (Cambridge: Polity).

Cook, R. (1988) 'Trends and needs in programming independent living', *Child Welfare*, Vol. LXVII, No. 6, November/December.

Cook, R. and Sedlak, A. (1993) 'Predictors of Outcomes for Youth Discharged from Foster Care', Unpublished paper presented at University of Illinois, September 1993.

Dalley, G. *Ideologies of Caring* (Basingstoke: Macmillan).

Department of Health (1991a) *Looking After Children: A Guide to the Action and Assessment Schedules* (London: HMSO).

Department of Health (1991b) *The Children Act 1989, Guidance and Regulations, Vol. 4, Residential Care* (London: HMSO).

Department of Health (1991c) *The Children Act 1989, Guidance and Regulations, Vol. 6, Children with Disabilities* (London: HMSO).

Department of Health (1991d) *Patterns and Outcomes in Child Placement* (London: HMSO).

Department of Health (1995) *Children Looked After by Local Authorities* (London: Department of Health).

DHSS (1985) *Social Work Decisions in Child Care* (London: HMSO).

Doyle, Paddy (1988) *The God Squad* (Great Britain: Corgi Books).

Fildes, V. (1988) *Wet Nursing : A History from Antiquity to the Present* (Oxford: Basil Blackwell).

Finkelhor, D., Hoteling, G., Lewis, I. and Smith, C. (1990) 'Sexual Abuse in a National Survey of Adult Men and Women: Prevalance Characteristics and Risk Factors', *Child Abuse and Neglect*, Vol. 14.

First Key (1987) *A Study of Black Young People Leaving Care* (Leeds: First Key).

First Key (1992) *A Survey of Local Authority Provision for Young People Leaving Care* (Leeds: First Key).

Fisher, M. et al. (1986) *In and Out of Care* (London: Batsford).

Fletcher-Campbell, F. (1990) 'In care? In school?', *Children and Society*, Vol. 4, No. 4, pp. 365–73.

Foucault, M.(1977a) *Discipline and Punish* (London: Allen and Lane).

Foucault, M.(1977b) *The Archaeology of Knowledge* (London: Tavistock).

Foucault, M.(1979) *The History of Sexuality, Vol. 1* (London: Allen and Lane).

Frost, N. and Stein, M. (1989) *The Politics of Child Welfare* (Hemel Hempstead: Harvester).

Frost, N. (1992) 'Implementing the Children Act, 1989' in Carter et al. (eds), *Changing Social Work and Social Welfare* (Milton Keynes: Open University).

Frost, N. (1997) 'Delivering family support', in Parton, N. (ed.), *Child Protection and Family Support* (London: Routledge).

Frost, N. and Harris, J. (1996) *Managing Residential Child Care* (Brighton: Pavilion).

Fraser, D. (1973) *The Evolution of the British Welfare State* (London: MacMillan).

Fry, E. (1992) 'Lost in transit', *Social Work Today*, 29 October.

Garnett, L. (1992) *Leaving Care and After* (London: National Children's Bureau).

Gil, D. (1982) 'Institutional Abuse of Children in Out-of-Home Care', *Children and Youth Services* [US], 4(1/2): 7–13.

Godek, S. (1976) *Leaving Care* (Ilford: Barnardo's).

Goffman, E. (1961) *Asylums* (Harmondsworth: Penguin).

Goffman, E. (1969) *The Presentation of Self in Everyday Life* (Harmondsworth: Pelican).

Grimwood, C. and Popplestone, R. (1993) *Women, Management and Care* (London: BASW/MacMillan).

Harris, J. and Kelly, D. (1991) *Management Skills in Social Care* (London: Ashgate).

Hawkins, P. and Shohet, R. (1989) *Supervision in the Helping Professions* (Milton Keynes: Open University Press).

Heath, A., Colton, M. and Aldgate, J. (1994) 'Failure to escape: A longitudinal study of foster children's educational attainment', *British Journal of Social Work*, Vol. 24, pp. 241–60.

Heath, A., Colton, M. and Aldgate, J. (1989) 'The educational progress of children in and out of foster care', *British Journal of Social Work*, Vol. 19, pp. 447–60.

Heywood, J. (1978) *Children in Care* (London: Routledge Kegan Paul).

HMSO (1991a) *Children in Public Care* (Sir William Utting) (London: HMSO).

HMSO (1991b) *Patterns and Outcomes in Child Placement* (London: HMSO).

HMSO (1992) *Choosing with Care, The Report of the Committee of Inquiry into the Selection, Development and Management of Staff in Children's Homes* (chair Norman Warner) (London: HMSO).

HMSO (1977) *People Like Us* (Sir William Utting) (London: HMSO).

Home Office (1968) *Children in Trouble* (London: HMSO).

Howe, E. (1992) *The Quality of Care (Howe Report)* (Luton: Local Government Management Board).

Hughes, W.H. (1985) *Report of the Committee of Inquiry into Children's Homes and Hostels* (Belfast: HMSO).

Jackson, S. (1989/9) 'Residential care and education', *Children and Society*, Vol. 4, pp. 335–50.

Jenks, C. (1996) *Childhood* (London: Routledge).

Jones, G. and Wallace, C. (1992) *Youth, Family and Citizenship* (Buckingham: Open University Press).

Jordan, L. (1992) 'Accommodation and aftercare: Provision for young people', *Journal of Child Law*, Vol. 4, No. 4.

Kadushin, A. (1976) *Supervision in Social Work* (New York: Columbia University Press).

Kahan, B. (1994) *Growing Up In Groups* (London: NISW).

Karban, K. and Mills, S. (1995) 'Testing the market – recruitment of qualified and experienced residential child care staff', *Journal of Practice and Staff Development*, 4(4): 21–33.

Kelly, L. (1989) *Surviving Sexual Violence* (London: Polity Press).

Kent, R. (1997) *Children's Safeguard Review* (Edinburgh: The Scottish Office).

Kirkwood, A. (1993) *The Leicestershire Inquiry 1992* (Leicestershire County Council).

Klein, M. (1985) *Where am I Going to Stay?* (Edinburgh: Scottish Council for the Single Homeless).

Lawson, E. (1985) *The Leeways Report* (London Borough of Lewisham).

Lee, P. and Pithers, D. (1980) 'Radical residential child care: Trojan horse or non-runner?' in Brake, M. and Bailey, R. (eds) *Radical Social Work and Practice* (London: Arnold).

Levy, A. and Kahan, B. (1991) *The Pindown Experience and the Protection of Children, The Report of the Staffordshire Child Care Inquiry* (Staffordshire County Council).

Logan, J. et al. (1996) *Confronting prejudice – Lesbian and Gay Issues in Social Work Education* (Aldershot: Arena).

Lyn-Cook, S. and Zutshi, H. (1993) *Action Guide for Developing and Using Statements of Purpose in Residential Care* (Luton: Local Government Management Board).

MacVeigh, J. (1982) *Gaskin* (London: Jonathan Cape).

Mallon, G.P. (1992) 'Gay and Nowhere to go: Assessing the Needs of Gay and Lesbian Adolescents in Out-of-Home Settings', *Child Welfare*, Vol. 71, No. 6.

Mallon, G.P. (1993) 'An Open Discussion about Gay and Lesbian Adolescents Out-of-Home Child Welfare Settings', *Daily Living*, Vol. 7, No. 2.

Mallon, G.P. (1994) 'Counselling Strategies with Gay and Lesbian Youths', *Journal of Gay and Lesbian Social Services*, Vol. 1, Nos 3/4.

Millham, S., Bullock, R., Hosie, K. and Haak, M. (1986) *Lost in Care* (Aldershot: Gower).

Mills, S. (1995) 'Creating a Safe Environment in Residential Child Care', in Stone and Mallender (1995).

Morrison, T. (1995) *Staff Supervision in Social Care* (London: Longman).

NACAB (1992) *Severe Hardship – CAB Evidence on Young People and Benefits* (London: NACAB).

National Children's Bureau (1992) *Child Facts*, 25 June (London: NCB).

NAYPIC (1983) *Sharing Care* (London: NAYPIC).

Nunno, M. and Rindfleisch, N. (1991) 'The Abuse of Children in Out of Home Care', *Children and Society*, Vol. 5, No. 4.

Osborne, S. (1992) 'The Quality Dimension: Evaluating Quality of Service and

Quality of Life in Human Services', *British Journal of Social Work*, Vol. 22.

Packman, J. (1981) *The Child's Generation* (London: Blackwell and Robertson).

Packman, J. (1986) *Who Needs Care?* (London: Blackwell).

Page, R. and Clarke, G. (eds) (1977) *Who Cares* (London: National Children's Bureau).

Parker, R. (1990) *Away From Home: A history of child care* (Ilford: Barnardo's).

Parker, R., Ward, H., Jackson, S., Aldgate, J. and Wedge, P. (eds) (1991) *Assessing Outcomes in Child Care* (London: HMSO).

Parton, N. (1985) *The Politics of Child Abuse* (London: Macmillan).

Payne, C. and Scott, T. (1982) *Developing Supervision of Teams in Field and Residential Social Work* (London: NISW).

Payne, M. (1982) *Working In Teams* (London: BASW/MacMillan).

Pearson, G. (1994) 'Youth, Crime and Society' in MacGuire, M., Morgan, R., Reiner, R. (eds) *The Oxford Handbook of Criminology* (Oxford: Oxford University Press).

Peters, T. and Waterman, R. (1983) *In Search of Excellence* (London: MacMillan).

Pinchbeck, I. and Hewitt, M. (1969) *Children in English Society* (London: Routledge, Kegan and Paul).

Pinkerton, J. and Kelly, G. (1986) 'Kincora Affair – the Aftermath', *Youth and Policy*, No. 17.

Piven, F. and Cloward, R.A. (1972) *Regulating the Poor* (London: Tavistock).

Pringle, K. (1990) *Managing to Survive* (Essex: Barnardo's).

Pringle, K. (1992) 'Gender Issues in the Sexual Abuse of Children by Welfare Professionals', paper given to 'Surviving Childhood Advisory Conference', Trinity College, Dublin.

Randall, G. (1988) *No Way Home* (London: Centrepoint).

Randall, G. (1989) *Homeless and Hungry* (London: Centrepoint).

Rees, G. (1993) *Hidden Truths: Young People's Experiences of Running Away* (London: Children's Society).

Richardson, A. and Ritchie, J. (1986) *Making the break: parent's views about adults with mental handicap leaving the parental home* (London: King's Fund).

Rowe, J. and Lambert, L. (1973) *Children Who Wait* (London: ABAA).

Rowe, J., Cain, H., Hundleby, M. and Keane, A. (1984) *Long Term Foster Care* (London: Batsford/BAAF).

Rowe, J., Hundleby, M. and Garnett, L. (1989) *Child Care Now* (London: Batsford/BAAF).

Senior, B. (1989) 'Residential Care: what hope for the future?' in Langan and Lee (eds), *Radical Social Work Today* (London: Unwin Hyman).

Simms, P. (1995) 'Measuring Quality in Residential Child Care' in Stone and Mallender (1995).

Sinclair, I. and Gibbs, I. (forthcoming) *Children's Homes: A Study in Diversity* (Chichester: Wiley).

Smith, C. (ed.) (1994) *Partnership in Action: Developing Effective Aftercare Projects* (Westerham: Royal Philanthropic Society).

Smythe, M. (1991) 'Press reporting of Kincora' in Franklin, B. and Parton, N. (eds) *Social Work, the Media and Public Relations* (London: Routledge).

Social Services Inspectorate (1985) *Inspection of Community Homes* (London: HMSO).

Social Services Inspectorate (1994) *Standards for Residential Child Care* (London: HMSO).

Social Services Inspectorate Wales (1991) *Accommodating Children. A review of Children's Homes in Wales* (Cardiff: Welsh Office).

Sone, K. (1994) 'Pick up the pieces', *Community Care*, 15–21 September.

SSAC (1992), *Social Security Advisory Committee, Eighth Report*, Social Services Committee, House of Commons (1984) *Second Report, Session 1983-84, Children in Care (The Short Report)* (London: HMSO).

Stein, M. (1983) 'Protest in Care' in Jordan, B. and Parton, N. (eds) *The Political Dimensions of Social Work* (Oxford: Blackwell).

Stein, M. (1990) *Living Out of Care* (Ilford: Barnardo's).

Stein, M. (1991) *Leaving Care and the 1989 Children Act, The Agenda* (Leeds: First Key).

Stein, M. (1993) *The Abuses and Uses of Residential Child Care in Surviving Childhood Adversity* (Dublin: Trinity College).

Stein, M. (1993) *Leaving Care, Research into Practice* (Leeds: First Key).

Stein, M. (1994) 'Leaving care, education and career trajectories', *Oxford Review of Education*, Vol. 20, No. 3, pp. 349–60.

Stein, M. (1997) *What Works in Leaving Care* (Barkingside: Barnardo's).

Stein, M. and Carey, K. (1986) *Leaving Care* (Oxford: Blackwell).

Stein, M. and Ellis, S. (1983) *Gizza Say* (London: NAYPIC).

Stein, M. and Maynard, C. (1985) *I've Never Been So Lonely* (London: NAYPIC).

Stockley, D. (1990) 'A Review of Literature and Statistics of Homelessness, Offending and Young People in Local Authority Care', unpublished paper, University of Surrey.

Stone, K. and Mallender, I. (1995) *Spinning Plates – Practice Teaching and Learning for the Residential Child Care Initiative* (London: CCETSW).

Stone, M. (1990) *Young People Leaving Care* (Redhill: The Royal Philanthropic Society).

Strathdee, R. and Johnson, M. (1994) *Out of Care and on the Streets. Young People, Care Leavers and Homelessness* (London: Centrepoint).

Streetwise National Coalition (1991) *A Research Study on Residential Care for Children and Adolescents in Ireland* (Dublin: Focus Point).

Turk, V. and Brown, H. (1992) *Sexual Abuse of Adults with Learning Difficulties* (Canterbury: Kent University).

Violence Against Children Study Group (1990) *Taking Child Abuse Seriously*, (London: Unwin Hyman).

Walton, R. and Elliot, D. (eds) (1980) *Residential Care: A Reader in Current Theory and Practice* (Oxford: Pergamon).

Webb, Sidney (1910) *English Poor Law Policy* (London: Longmans).

Weiner, R. (1992) *Team Building and the Art of Team Doctoring* (Leeds: University of Leeds).

Westcott, H. and Clement, M. (1992) *Experience of Child Abuse in Residential Care and Educational Placements* (London: NSPCC).

White Paper (1987) The Law on Child Care and Family Services, Cmnd 62 (London: HMSO).

Who Cares? Trust (1993) *Not Just a Name: The Views of Young People in Foster and Residential Care* (London: National Consumer Council).

Williams, G. and McCreadie, J. (1992) *Ty Mawr Community Homes Inquiry* (Gwent County Council, Wales).

Young Homelessness Group (1991) *Carefree and Homeless* (London: Young Homelessness Group).

Index

For Product Safety Concerns and Information please contact our EU representative GPSR@taylorandfrancis.com Taylor & Francis Verlag GmbH, Kaufingerstraße 24, 80331 München, Germany

Printed and bound by CPI Group (UK) Ltd, Croydon, CR0 4YY

08/05/2025

01864401-0001